SAVING MY A.

A Story of Cancers, Colons & Singapore Noodles

By

Mark Davies

Published By: Mark Davies

This work has been registered with the Writers' Copyright Association (www.wcauk.com).

Registration No:C102653

Acknowledgements:

I would like to extend my sincere thanks to the staff of all the hospitals that I have visited over the past few years.

A special mention to the staff of Homerton Hospital & St Bartholomew's (Barts) Hospital in London, The Royal Liverpool Hospital & The Clatterbridge Centre of Oncology on the Wirral.

Special Acknowledgements:

I would like to offer my unwavering gratitude and support to the two men, Dr Sun Myint and Mr Michael Hershman, who put their reputations and careers on the line to help save my life and my arse. Thank you.

What Can I say?

My recovery & this book have only been possible because of the love and support of my Mum & Dad, my partner Rachel, and the rest of my family and friends. Without whom, I would have gone as quietly bonkers as I'm sure that I have made them.
Xx

**For Nana & Grandad -
Who make life look so easy**

SAVING MY ARSE - Chapter list:

I must not fear.
Fear is the mind-killer.
Fear is the little-death that brings total obliteration.
I will face my fear.
I will permit it to pass over me and through me.
And when it has gone past I will turn the inner eye to see its path.
Where the fear has gone there will be nothing.
Only I will remain.

Paul Atreides - Bene Gesserit Litany against fear.
Dune – Frank Herbert

*****

DON'T PANIC

Written on the cover of the Hitchhikers Guild to the Galaxy
– Douglas Adams

*****

Do not drink pure orange juice when receiving chemotherapy; it will give you the worst arse of your life!

Observations from a toilet cubicle in North London -
Mark Davies

2am Sunday 1st of June 2003 BC
(Before Cancer)

2am Sunday 1st of June 2003 BC
(Before Cancer)

CHAPTER 1: THE MORNING AFTER THE NIGHT BEFORE.

It was the very early hours of a Sunday morning. The air was exceptionally warm for early June, warning of the scorcher to come later that summer. A steady breeze carried the triumphant chants of late night revellers returning from the area's numerous bars and clubs and the shrill of a distant siren answering the call of another emergency. In a quiet apartment complex just up from Islington not much was moving – even the twenty-four hour security guard had dozed off in his little room. Above the din of silence a low, almost inhuman groan could be heard. Listening closer you could just about believe that the sound might turn out to be that of a male. Even closer and jumbled words become apparent, like the rantings of a madman clearly in pain. It is nearly 3 am and something or someone is clearly awake in the apartments known as Red Square, and all is not well (said Rhubarb to Custard – sorry couldn't resist). Listening still closer, you can hear that the screams are emanating from a bathroom.

"SHIT, FUCKITY SHIT SHIT – OH MY GOOD LORD LET IT BE OVER! This is taking the piss – I am *never* going to eat Singapore Noodles again."

Who is this unfortunate? This tortured soul (well arse anyway!)? ... My name is Mark Davies and at that time I'm thirty-one years old. It's the 1st of June and I am on the bog *again* for the third time that night, dropping off a load of very angry kids at a very small pool. Let me give you some background on our presently encamped hero. I'm of average height – five foot ten and a half – admittedly a tad over weight at just under fifteen stone – I much prefer the phrase "compact" to fat. I did smoke – only about ten to fifteen a day, though this obviously doesn't include when going out for a drink when that can easily double. In terms of drink I think roughly ten to fifteen pints a week should cover it. I had also been known to have the odd toke of the occasional "herbal" cigarette.

My major problem was eating the wrong foods at the wrong times, and that was due mainly to the long hours that I'd work, like a large number of people who work in the city. My lifestyle was not the best in the world and hadn't been for quite some time. I went to university in Bournemouth – good beach. After graduating in 1995 I stayed on in Bournemouth and pretty much continued the student lifestyle, whilst working in various service industries and pursuing my own retail concept, which unfortunately I never got the financial backing for. At the end of 1997 I realised that if I continued the way I was going I would never get out of the rather drunken rut that I had found myself in, so I upped and left everything, and moved to London. I stayed with friends until I started with a direct sales company and quickly got promoted to assistant management. One of the downsides of promotion was that I spent the next three to four years racing around the country, running offices for other people, whilst working twelve to fourteen hours a day, and living in shared company houses with up to eight to ten people at a time. This was not a major problem in itself; however it did result in my having a minor heart scare in the summer of 2000 after my office in Portsmouth was closed owing to organisational product changes.

I was given the responsibility of developing a new product range in the London area in February 2001. I have never worked so hard in my life, although this led to the setting up of my own company the following October and meeting my current girlfriend Rachel who lives with myself and another workmate; things were rather hectic. In a nutshell, for the best part of a decade I hadn't really been treating my body as a temple, but much more like a bus shelter.

At the time this story starts I am running a small sales office in east London and things are not "hunky dory" to say the least. The previous weekend had been our organisation's R&R weekend in Koz. Whilst it was a giggle, I found it all a bit false having to be ultra-positive when things were not. It had been a hectic six to eight months. I had opened a second office in Glasgow, sending a very young but talented assistant manager to run it. Unfortunately by February, owing to supplier problems again and forever changing products, I had to leave my London office under the care of another manager to go and give her a hand. This again wasn't a problem; Glasgow rocks! However, the living out of hotels whilst working fourteen hours a day was hardly conducive to healthy stress free living. I spent about two months flying up and down from London to Glasgow, and during this time the office in London suffered and I got more and more stressed and increasingly tired. By the end of April I took the decision to close Glasgow and consolidate the London base. This little venture had cost me over £30,000, which was most of the savings in the company; I shrugged it off, saying: "Well hey, I've never had £30,000 to lose before." Post-heart scare I had forced myself to chill out a bit more. I had to change my general outlook on life and realised that I could not do everything myself and started to undertake things with a more measured approach, such as the way I dealt with problems and my expenditure of time and effort. I realised that there are two types of problems: (1) things you can do something about, and (2) things you can't. A lot of people expend far too much energy on the latter and not the former.

It was June and the start of our busiest time of the year and try as I might I was finding it hard to concentrate. I was always tired and just could not motivate myself, or my guys. I was going to the bathroom a lot – by that I mean at least eight to ten times a day. I was having occasional stomach cramps, which felt like my intestines were being used as a stress ball. In addition to this I would also occasionally find a little bit of blood spotting when having a poo. I can only relate it to "period pains of the bum". On top of that I had noticed, well actually my girlfriend Rachel had noticed, that I had become, shall we say, a little windy. Having managed to completely sidestep the whole leg waxing, moisturising '90s man thing, I wasn't unduly worried by the odd unintentional gaseous outburst. In all fairness though, by this time I had seriously gone past the odd "expulsion" to full on "anal Tourette's".

These symptoms had been going on for at least six to eight weeks, but when you're running round like a headless chicken the tendency is to ignore them. It was probably just a bit of food poisoning or it could have been just stress related; eating too late can also cause these problems. There is never a good time to have time off when you have responsibilities. You know the deal: when you're "hot" everyone is your friend, and when you're not well – we'll do lunch. So anyway, the point of this little tirade is that, I was tired, yes. Having an affair with the bathroom suite, maybe; but I "Didn't have a Scooby" that there was actually anything wrong with me. However, after another eventful Saturday night/Sunday morning in pain on the loo, I thought it was high time I got myself down the docs – at some juncture anyway. Sunday came and went, and I felt so ropey that I didn't even want the rest of the Chinese for breakfast, which is serious in my book (bi-product of spending too long at university). As usual by the evening I was feeling fine again and I'd put the previous night's rear-ended fireworks down as extra chillies on the noodles and nothing more. Come Monday morning June 2nd my stomach had settled down but I just couldn't get motivated and decided to throw what turned out to be the most important sickie in my life, and took myself off to the doctors. Funny really how life works out isn't it? If I had not been completely knackered and rung in; if I had not ignored the usual arm-twisting and guilt complexes about being a bad example, blah-blah-blah! I might not be writing this at all.

So, I manage to blag my way into the local surgery and see a lovely lady called Doctor Young. And this is where the fun starts! I had no idea what was up with me; in fact I was pretty sure that there was nothing wrong in the slightest. I'd been working too hard, eating rubbish at all the wrong times and was under a lot of stress as I'd just been told that I wasn't able to take wages anymore and had to generate my income directly from personal sales; oh joy! I was convinced that at the absolute worst I might have a small ulcer. Doctor Young listened to my tale of woe (had to lay it on thick so I didn't look like a big girl's blouse).

The symptoms were as follows:

- Increased toilet activity,
- Random stomach cramps,
- Slight weight loss (which considering the amount of time on the bog is not surprising),
- Always feeling tired/unable to get motivated, and a
- Minimal amount of blood – sometimes.

The good doctor listened, felt my lower stomach, which was nice, and out of the blue suggested that I should see a specialist. Cool, I thought. That's got to be worth another day off at least, a real live specialist. As you can tell I was pretty blasé about the whole thing. This is why Dr

Young deserves a lot of praise, because all joking aside she could well have saved my life by being so professional and on the ball, although she did have cold hands. And so the good doctor and I parted company and I went back to work as normal and all but forgot about the upcoming appointment. A couple of weeks later a letter arrived confirming an appointment with a Dr Ballinger at Homerton Hospital in Hackney on June 24th. Throughout this time I cannot stress enough that I did not have the faintest of ideas as to what was wrong and continued along my own little path, completely oblivious of the "Tumour" that was growing inside. As far as I was concerned I just had the shits.

CHAPTER 2: BOLDLY GOING ...

Why is it that when you make a doctors appointment you feel like crap, but by the time you get round to seeing the doctor you're absolutely fine? I had gone back to work and all was well with the world. I was now feeling fine within myself, still a bit tired, and was frequenting the loo more than normal, but all in all not too bad. So by the time I got to the hospital it was more a case of going over what had been wrong previously which I felt bad about, because I felt that the doctors time would be better used with someone who was actually ill.

The big day arrived. I went to work in the morning, as per usual, set the guys up for the day, did a couple of training meetings and some early interviews and then off to the hospital. I have to admit that I was pleasantly surprised by the hospital itself. Going by the amount of stick the NHS gets I was expecting a nightmare. It was spotless, open and easily accessible and most importantly everyone was really nice. However, it is important that when visiting the doctors or the hospital that you go prepared – take a book! If the saying "good things come to those who wait" were true, hospitals would be the happiest places on the planet. I'd just started reading a fantasy by a writer called Terry Brooks and his Shannara series (very LOTR Dwarfs and the like). There are twelve in the series and now I've read them all, plus all of the Frank Herbert "DUNE" books. Trust me, there are only so many copies of Gardeners' World from the 90s, or Anglers Friend you can read before your brain melts and your mind wants to crawl off into a corner and have a little cry. You have been warned! Anyway I digress.

My name was called and I entered the inner sanctum. Dr Ballinger was, as you would expect, a very smart-looking woman. She sat me down and started with the basic information: Address, age, took my height, weight and so forth, then down to the questions about my symptoms. Now one of the problems with men is that whilst we may claim that we are dying when nothing is really wrong with us, when something is seriously wrong we are often completely oblivious. Looking back I should have taken the fact that she was actually listening to what I was saying a little more seriously – she hadn't once said "take two of these twice a day and ring if there's a problem". I had no idea what was to come. The chat went on for about twenty minutes and then she told me to go into the adjacent room because she needed to examine me. Still not a clue! The examination room was small and painted in that NHS off-white that makes you feel like you are inside an egg. I hopped onto the bed and waited. Dr Ballinger came in and asked me to pull down my trousers. Not a Scooby! I lay back and she felt my stomach, she umm-ed and ahh-ed a bit. Then she uttered the words that I would come to hear a lot more and would come to dread:

"Could you roll onto your left side, pull down your underwear and pull your knees up towards your chest." Then, at last my brain decided to join the party and inform me of what was about to happen, "I'm just going to examine the inside of your **back port**." Back port? Back *fucking* port. I thought this was going to be another tummy tickling session, so what is all this back port business? The only words that sprang to my mind as I watched her lube her fingers were, "Shouldn't we at least do dinner first, or a show?" I whimpered whilst looking over my right shoulder. As she approached with a wry smile (she probably didn't have a wry smile at all), I was a tad concerned. I had stopped looking at her and was completely focused on what looked like an abnormally long index finger, like a distant relation of ET's but without the light on the end. My mind was screaming

MORE LUBE! And then she did a Captain Kirk and "Boldly Went"! Well, she definitely examined my back port all right. I thought her finger was going to come out of my mouth at one point. Not good, not good *at all*. After what felt like hours, but was probably seconds, she withdrew, smiled, and told me to just "pop" my clothes back on and come through to the other room. She turned and left me there, half naked, abused, traumatised. Well OK, it wasn't that bad. But even so it was a bit of a shock, I *can* tell you!

I dressed and minced back into the main room and sat gingerly down, like the chair was alive and out to get me. "OK" she said. That was not enough information for me at that point, but she did proceed. The doctor said that I would need another appointment, but before that could happen I would have to have a Colonoscopy. I have to admit that I wasn't really listening at that time, as my mind had gone off to find another little corner. As I was leaving, I just sort of smiled and asked jokingly if the second appointment would involve anymore "back port" action, and this time I got what was definitely a wry smile.

Oh Joy!

I feel that at this point in the story I should just give a brief overview of what is going on medically. The reason for this is that I did not know anything about the procedures prior to my illness but I wish that I had. So as Jennifer Aniston says in those dodgy shampoo ads: "Now for the science"!

If a GP or hospital specialist is concerned after they perform the traditional "tour de Back Port", that further *investigation* is required; they will recommend one or more options from a list of several diagnostic procedures. The three most commonly used of these are:

Proctoscopy/Sigmoidoscopy – The most obvious way to find something is to look for it. This however has the slight problem in that what they are looking for is several inches up one's arse. So its camera up the arse time I'm afraid. The proctoscope is only short and is designed to look just into the rectum; the sigmoidoscope is longer and is to look further along the large bowel. It has a small light on the inside to allow the doctors to see any abnormal areas. I find it strange that most of the texts that I've read about this sort of procedure only ever mention the length of the "soon to be shoved up your jacksie" thingy. However, as my girlfriend keeps telling me it's the girth not the length that matters (of course she could just be trying to make me feel better). So in real life terms the proctoscope is about the size of a Smartie tube, and the sigmoidoscope with its lights inside looks like a sodding lightsaber. That aside, with a healthy dose of KY, it will be uncomfortable at worst and you will be able to hobble slowly home afterwards.

Barium Enema – I don't know about you but this just sounds bad. I never had to have this procedure so it's "just the facts Jack!" Essentially it's just a special X-ray and will take place in hospital. Now because this is an X-ray you will be required to drink a lot of liquids and take some laxative the day before. This is to ensure that the bowel is empty so that a clear picture can be seen with the X-ray. Remember that X-ray pictures are not always the clearest of images and the last thing you need is to be rushed into surgery with a malignant piece of sweetcorn! Now, I will try not to neg you out, but this is what happens. Just before the procedure a bowel wash-out is required; essentially you lie on your side while a nurse passes a small tube up the bum and then water is passed through the tube and the patient is asked to hold it in for a couple of minutes before going to the loo. A bit like gargling with your bum. Air, as well as the barium, is then passed up the pipe to expand the bowel to get a clearer picture. This is uncomfortable and you may want someone to pick you up from the hospital. Side-effects are minimal; poo might be turned white for a couple of days – this is just the barium washing out the system – and some mild constipation may be experienced.

There are other methods such as the Ultrasound Scan and a CT or CAT scan. These, however, will be explained in due course, but first off to the Colonoscopy.

CHAPTER 3: AND SO IT BEGINS …

The Colonoscopy, also known as having a rather large tube shoved all the way up where the sun don't shine, was scheduled for Thursday 10th July. I felt it was high time to call in the experts, and so rang my mum. It is important to realise that mums *know all*! Apart from developing the uncanny ability to make really good roast potatoes, mums are also very adept at doing all the panicking for you, allowing you to continue with your everyday life unabated. I am very fortunate to have the relationship with my mum that I do. My parents separated when I was eight, so although my dad was still around a lot and they still have a good relationship (Dad came to my mum's wedding to my stepdad, Geoff – how cool is that), it was still my mum who predominately brought up my younger brother, Ben, and myself. Although I left home at the age of nineteen, she is still the only person who can get away with saying, " You're *not* going out like that are you?"

So I left my mum to worry while I waited for the appointment. In case you were unaware the colon is also known as the large bowel. The idea behind the Colonoscopy is to try and inspect all the way up and along the large bowel to visually assess any potential problems. To make sure that this is as easy as possible I had to have a special *low residue* diet to clean out the entire lower bowel. This was a four-day regime, which I started on the Sunday. The diet reduces the amount of solid food intake over the four days, so that by the time you're in hospital things are as clean as a whistle, in an up your bum sort of way. *If you don't like Cup a Soups this is going to be a really boring four days.* On the day before the Colonoscopy I had to go onto a pretty much 100% liquid diet and I had to take a pretty hardcore laxative called 'Picolax'. To be honest I had never taken any type of laxative before. I'm of the "five pints of Cobra and a

Madras will pretty much shift anything" school of thought, so in a perverse way I was quite looking forward to the whole thing.

On the Wednesday morning I was up nice and early and prepared for a day of hardcore toilet time. Luckily the flat I shared with my girlfriend and another friend had a downstairs loo. This might seem a bit of a weird revelation but believe me with Picolax you will need to know the exact toilet dash time. It is very important that, should you ever have to undergo this procedure, a lot of liquid be consumed throughout as going to the toilet this much will cause dehydration. It might just be me but I thought this Picolax stuff was great. I could imagine it being a tad uncomfortable if I had been eating as normal, but since there was nothing really left in me at all, it was just, well, pretty funny. The effects are that anything inside you makes a break for it, and anything that goes in afterwards will also want to leave just as quickly. I could sit on the loo and have a drink and have it come out the other end almost immediately. I was literally laughing at this because it is a very strange sensation which felt like I was being washed throughout my body, and made me feel, for want of a better phrase, "clean on the inside". For some reason I got the urge to share this experience so I rang Rachel (my girlfriend) from the toilet. Whilst I thought that this might be an amusing distraction from her working day, Rachel however could only really manage an "urrrrrr that's not nice!" Well I was amused even if no one else was.

The day arrived and I was off to hospital for a date with a hose. A quick taxi over to Homerton, and into the hospital I went, alone – no fear! Upon recollection it might well have been advisable to take someone along. I didn't have to wait too long before my name was called. I slipped into the "Oh so sexy" hospital gown and waited. After a few minutes a doctor came and introduced himself, and explained the upcoming procedure to me. I have to admit to a certain level of trepidation at this point. Having someone shove a long thin tube up my back door was not on my "to do" list for 2003. I went into the operating room and hopped on the bed and readied myself. A small catheter was inserted into a vein on the back of my hand, into which a mild relaxant would be administered before the procedure would start.

When I'm nervous I try to make light of the situation, and have the tendency to talk to anyone and everyone. However when I asked for a *lot* of relaxant I was not joking, although by this point the doctor might well have thought that I was already on all sorts of drugs given that I was twittering on like a record on 78 rpm. Luckily he obliged me, probably just to shut me up, and it was good stuff whatever it was; I didn't really feel the tube go in. To explain, the tube being used looks like one of those secret spy optical fibres that are used in the movies to look through grates or vents, etc. So the intrusion was not as bad as I had first expected until, that is, they turned the air on. The tube was lit but not very thick so they had to inflate the whole of my colon to get the best picture. I started to watch this journey into the unknown on the mini TV next to the bed, but the increase in air pressure up my arse completely put me off my stride. The drugs where beginning to take full control of my head, but up my arse all was not well. Imagine the worst fart that you could muster, reverse it, and methodically push it all the way back to your stomach. I *soooooo* needed to let rip but just could not explain that to my body. I have no idea how long I was on the bed but I had to say something: "I'm just gonna go for a little walk," I announced to the doctor. This obviously wasn't going to happen, as apart from the fact that the tube was still "boldly going", I had been given a bucket-load of relaxant and my legs were having none of it.

So in true pioneering spirit I tried, failed, whimpered and lay back down again mumbling "I'll go in a minute then!"

Then as soon as it was started it was over. The tube was reclaimed and I was led away to a recovery cubicle and instructed to lie down and rest for at least an hour. As soon as the nurse had left, I was out of there. The pain is like the worst trapped wind you can imagine. I could just about dress myself, whilst venting excess air left right and centre. I staggered out of the hospital and rang for a cab. I was doubled over walking like a pregnant ET. The cabbie who came to collect me was the same one who had brought me to the hospital a couple of hours before; God only knows what he must have thought seeing this lolloping image approaching the car, bent over, face etched in pain and determination. I collapsed into the front seat, and managed only "Home James".

Once home I went up to my room, took off my trousers, clambered onto my bed, lay on my back, brought my knees up à la birthing delivery position and farted the best, longest, most unbelievably welcome fart of my life. I groaned with unabashed pleasure; you know the saying, "better out than in"? Well they are not fucking wrong I can tell you. I lay there for over an hour, farting, aching, and breathing like I was in a lamas class; it was like having a large air baby. I must stress that you must not under any circumstances attempt to drive home after this procedure; try to have someone there or organise a cab. Public transport might not be advisable as you will not be the most popular person on the bus or tube, although you would create quite a large seating space for yourself. By the time Rachel got home I was fine again, although I did keep up the pretence of discomfort for the rest of the night; my arse and I needed comforting. Next day I was back at work as per, and put it to the back of my mind along with the next appointment, which was almost two weeks away.

During this time the symptoms persisted, although I still had no idea as to what the problem was. I was beginning to get the feeling that my original diagnosis of an ulcer may well have been correct. This was a bit of a revelation because as I mentioned I wasn't completely convinced that I had anything that a bit of a rest, less beer and junk food wouldn't cure.

On the following Tuesday my confusion deepened. Whilst at work I received a phone call from the hospital asking me to come in on that Friday for a CT scan, just four days before my next scheduled appointment. This information was obviously passed on to all concerned parties, i.e. mum and Rachel; they worried, I went for the scan, perfect! So once again I found myself at the hospital and at the mercy of yet more anally obsessed doctors and nurses. Luckily for this procedure, 99% of all liquid in-take is through more traditional orifices. As opposed to four days of fasting with the Colonoscopy, this was only four hours – no problem! Once in the waiting area I was given about a pint and a half of weird tasting orange squash which I was assured would help in the procedure. This liquid apparently shows up during the scan, which is in essence a fancy X-ray.

Note: For asthmatics, do mention that you are a sufferer to the nurses as the weird orange stuff may cause a slight reaction. An hour or so later I'm on my back, laced with juice, being passed through a large doughnut! It was all over within half an hour and I was out and back in work before you could say: "Phew! Was that you? No! Must have been me then!"

Next stop was my appointment on 22nd July, when all would be revealed, and I'd have a week's holiday to get over my upcoming ulcer, or possibly IBS as some people were beginning to speculate.

CHAPTER 4: THE BIG DAY.

On the Monday evening I received a call from my mum asking me if I wanted her to come down for the results of the tests. Now I don't know about your parents, but when my mum asks for something it generally means it is going to happen whether I want it to or not. I mentioned the fact that I was the managing director of my own company; I mentioned the fact that I was thirty-one; I also mentioned the fact that I'd being going to the doctors "all by myself" for a very long time. My mum mentioned the fact that she was still my mum and that she would see me at Euston station at about twelve. It's nice to be asked though!

So, Mum in tow, we made our way from the train station to the hospital.

We traversed the waiting area, I registered at reception and we took our seats. I still had not really started to worry about all this as I was still convinced that I was pretty much fine, so was chatting to Mum about work developments etc. when my name was called. We both stood up, I looked over to Mum and she sat down again, "I'll wait here then." I smiled, said that I thought I could cope, and followed the nurse though to the consultation room of Dr Ballinger. I knocked and went in. In the room there were two other people – one was evidently a junior doctor and the other was a young dark haired lady called Alex who I was informed was the hospital registrar.

"Ooo! A crowd" I said. "You guys hunt in packs now do you?" (Remember the nerves and talking bit.)

"Please take a seat Mr Davies." Once the introductions were over I sat and went Bugs for a second.

"So! What's up Doc?" I said, smiling inanely.

"You have adenocarcinoma of the colorectal region."

"Eh?"

CHAPTER 5: YOU HAVE CANCER MR. DAVIES!

"You have cancer Mr Davies!"

"Oh. OK! So what do we do about it?"

Tuesday 22nd of July 2003 AD
(After Diagnosis)

CHAPTER 6: THE FIRST DAY OF THE REST OF MY LIFE

Faith! (*Noun* 1: complete trust or confidence. 2: belief in a religion. 3: a system of religious belief.)

Should you ever be in this situation, I believe it is your faith that will steer you in the appropriate direction. People seem to want to live with faith, but die for religion, which can't be right. Faith and religion are, from my point of view, completely different. I am not a religious person. I have been to church only two or three times in my entire life and that includes my christening. I get a real case of the "heebie-geebies" (bit like Damien) if I even go into a church. However, I feel that I have faith, or trust or confidence, in what I believe. And what is it that I believe in? Well for want of a better word: "Me". When we are told that we have cancer, each of us will react in a different manner. Some will break down; some may be hysterical; some may go into shock or denial. I believe that when our time is up, it's up. There is nothing that you can do about it. I also believe that there is a lot more to life than can be measured by science or present schools of thought. Just because I don't put a name to it doesn't mean that I don't believe in a grand design or anything. I have a fatalist view that what happens, happens for a reason (not always a recognisable reason I grant you), and it's our own decisions after the fact that makes us who we are – for example my parents divorced and I still managed to mug zero grannies nor steal any cars.

I believe in the power of the individual, the power of the mind to deal with almost anything that is thrown at us. I never felt that it was my time to die, and therefore had a sense of "fait accompli"; the gauntlet had been thrown down and it was up to me to pick it up and get on with it. Of course I am writing this retrospectively, and therefore have had time to assess my feelings on the whole matter. At the time my mind simply reacted with "shit".

"You have cancer Mr Davies!" I had always, in a macabre way, imagined what I would do if I was told that I had cancer. We have all seen it on TV, in films or even in those charity adverts. What would you do? Several strange thoughts hurried through my mind, apart from "shit". Time seemed to slow to almost a complete stop like Bullet Time from the Matrix, as all these thoughts just popped in there: *"Mum is gonna kill me"*; *"Not an ulcer then"*; I even thought about a question I was asked in an interview once, about what to write for your own epitaph *"I told them it was more than a headache"* (arse ache in my case); *What am I going to tell Rachel?* Etc. I fixed my stare on the doctor and simply and very calmly said, "OK. So what do we do about it?"

   This probably wasn't the sort of reaction that she was expecting. Alex shifted slightly; the junior doctor had his head slightly bowed as if not wanting to make eye contact. I felt very calm, a lot calmer than I would have thought. I went into work mode: here is the problem – how do we deal with it? All I wanted now was to be educated about the situation; arm myself with knowledge if you like. The cancer was at the end of the colon, towards the top end of the rectum. Dr Ballinger brought out the file and went through the details with me. The tumour had probably been growing for nine months or more, which would explain why I had been feeling so tired since around Christmas. I was shown a couple of photos of the tumour, which I thought looked like an upturned strawberry blancmange. The strange thing was that the tumour had an ulcer smack-bang in its middle, which was slightly raised like a bald man looking over a wall. The tumour was a couple of centimetres across and was, apparently, poorly differentiated. I still don't know what that means exactly, but it wasn't good because this meant that it was a killer and would spread more quickly than your standard tumour.

"Glad to hear that I haven't got just a normal boring tumour" I joked. No one laughed. "I'll get my coat!" I thought. This was all getting a bit too much for me to take in. My mind desperately wanted to find its favourite small corner, but I was not letting it.

Then I remembered my mum out in the waiting room. I could deal with the cancer, but what I couldn't deal with was telling my mum. I mean what do you say? I was fine, but I knew that I couldn't tell her myself. I wanted her to be as up to speed, if not more so, than I was. I had already decided that I was going to have to go and get really drunk so one of us would have to remember the details. It is advisable that you have someone for the diagnosis because however you cope with the initial "okey-dokey then!" a lot of information will be fired at you and you will just not remember it all. "I have a favour to ask: my mum insisted on coming down for the results. She is in reception; could you tell her please?" Straight away Alex and Dr Ballinger responded with a resounding "yes – no problem". So gratefully I went too retrieve my mum from the waiting area.

I walked into the reception and just beckoned her to follow me. "Everything OK?" she asked. "Err well not quite; I'll let the doctors explain." I know – what a bottler but what can you do? I followed her into the doctor's room and performed the introductions. I let Mum sit next to the doctor as I lent casually against the wall. Mum listened to the doctor explain what the situation was. No hysterics. No blubbing. Mum just sat there nodding, taking the information in whilst I watched and listened in a kind of stunned silence. "I thought as much," said my mum. "I was pretty sure after you called him in for the

CT scan!"

"*What!*" I thought.

"I thought that with his symptoms and the extra care that you where taking that it might be cancer."

"What?" I now managed to say. "Could have let me in on it then!" I exclaimed.

"He has a tendency to hide his feelings with humour," said my mum.

"We had noticed," said Alex.

"So what's next?" asked Mum.

Great, now I'm being talked about in the third person as if I'm not even here I thought. Although now aware that I had cancer, I had completely forgotten to ask what was going to happen to me.

"What is the prognosis doctor?" asked my mum. Even though it sounds like dialogue from a dodgy daytime hospital soap, it was a fair and valid question. Whilst I was convinced that I was not going to die, it would be nice to hear if the doctors agreed. "Not completely clear at the moment due to the positioning of the tumour within the colorectal region; and of course the fact that it's poorly differentiated would suggest that it will probably spread quickly, if it hasn't already," said the doctor.

"So what is next?" asked my mum. "I know what's next for me," I thought, "Stella and lots of it!" Next, from a non-beer point of view, was an appointment with the head surgeon in two days, a Mr Lunnis back there at Homerton. We thanked the team and left.

"You OK?" I asked Mum.

"Been better," Mum replied. "What do you want to do now?" she asked.

"Well I've just been told that I've got cancer, so I think I should go and get some ciggies and we should go to the pub and get drunk!" As I have already mentioned, my relationship with my mum is a good one. She is one of these people who could organise even the English footy team into a recognisable shape. She worked in the service industries through most of my childhood managing the restaurant at Chester racecourse as well as some top northwest hotels before moving to be operations manager for an FE college called Burton Manor. I knew that me being ill would be devastating to her and the rest of my family, but I also knew that my mum often works on the same "if I can't do anything about it why panic" type mentality. I also knew that she was a bit of a fan of the saying "to be forewarned is to be forearmed" and would be all over this situation as soon as she got home. Organising is what she does and if that means organising information and advice, then that is what will happen, in buckets. This was a good thing, as I already knew that I was going to the pub and at least one of us should be moderately sensible about the whole cancer thing.

Fifteen minutes later we were in The Living Rooms in Islington (top bar to drink in as it's got very comfortable chairs and sofas, quality background music, and very good staff – which is nice!). No Stella unfortunately but a pint of export lager and a large chaser would suffice for the time being. Mum went for the vodka and tonic option. I was aware that at some point I would have to try to mentally work through this, and worst of all I had to try and work out the best way to tell Rachel, the other lady in my life.

It was quite a surreal afternoon of drinking. I had just been given the worst news of my life so far, but both my mum and myself were completely calm. We talked about the problem, decided that it could be dealt with, and that there was absolutely no point in panicking. The full details of the prognosis would only become clearer after the appointment with the consultant surgeon in two days' time. That however did not help me with having to tell Rachel.

Rachel at the time worked in the same office as I did, which was good because I had friends there who could keep an eye on her for me. So I rang my friend and housemate Jon (also known as Jonk) from my mobile, at the office first. I explained the situation to him, asked where Rachel was and whom she was with, and made sure that he would go up to where Rachel was before I rang her. I left the quietness of the bar, went outside through the open front shutter doors and rang her mobile number. What is it about talking on a mobile that means that you find yourself pacing up and down wherever you happen to find yourself at the time.

"Hi honey – how's work going?"

"Same ol' same ol'. How was the doctors?" Bugger straight in there. I was sort of hoping to skirt round the whole cancer thing for a while.

"Well, there's some good news and some not so good news!" Here goes nothing …

"On the plus side it wasn't IBS or an ulcer, on the downside I've got cancer of the colon or bowel or something like that. But I'm FINE and I'm in the pub with Mum having quite a lot of beer – me not Mum obviously. She's on the vodka!" The silence on the other end of the phone was the killer – even though it was only seconds it seemed like ages. I wanted more than anything to be telling her face-to-face not over the phone but these were the cards and this is the way that they were being dealt. Rachel went with the, "Are you OK?" Which is a fair question, but then I could feel her mentally chastise herself, "*Of course you're not OK –*

you've got cancer." There was no easy way for me to tell people that I had got cancer, not because of own condition but because of the distress that it caused in others that cared about me. I found as I grew more used to having cancer that I welcomed questions about my situation as opposed to the uncomfortable silences that I would get when I was first diagnosed. Education equals motivation; the more I talked about it to people the better they understood and were cool about it.

The rest of the details of that conversation, along with a lot of the aspects of that day are still surprisingly vague. I don't remember them in any particular order or indeed if they really happened at all. This was owing to the fact that I was probably in a mild state of shock and that there was a significant amount of alcohol involved. We talked for a while and I assured her that I was fine, which I was, and that I would talk to her more when I got home. From what I remember Rachel was pretty calm about the whole thing; of course she probably didn't want to go "gaga" over the phone and upset the situation further. I would come to rely on that strength later on during this rather strange chapter in my life.

Well that was the hardest part of the day over with as far as I was concerned; hearing the bad news for myself was nowhere near as bad as having to pass that information on to those whom I care about, and don't want to upset. As it happened I would be able to achieve a "full house" in the bad news game of life because Mum reminded me that I was due to meet up with my dad later that day. By some strange coincidence (remember what I said about things happening as if by design) Dad had booked into a London hotel for a mini-break with my step-mum Jean and my two step nieces, whom I had never actually met, Kirsty, ten, and Charlotte, thirteen. I dropped off my mum at Euston station at around seven and walked down to my Dad's hotel near the National Museum, off Russell Square.

The hotel was like the Tardis, with a fairly small fascia but pretty large on the inside. I went straight to the bar to wait for Dad, who was mentally torturing the girls by dragging them round the various museums that were on his "holiday agenda" list. I was barely halfway through my first pint when they all arrived. Whilst the relationship with my mother is more like friends than just parent/child, I'd never really had that with Dad. The fact that this was the first time that I was meeting my step niece's kind of makes that point. Saying that, I am not renowned for being the most emotional of people, something my ex-girlfriends would definitely testify to. Dad, Jean and the girls came through to the bar got their drinks and we all grabbed a table and started with the chitchat. To be honest it was quite good fun.

Dad and Jean are the grandparents of the girls, which meant that I had a captive young audience to recount amusing stories about the afore mentioned grandparents. I like kids. Well that's not completely true – I like some kids, and Kirsty and Charlotte are great kids. Polite, alert, very intelligent – not in a swotty way but in a quick-to-pick-things-up sort of way. Plus they laughed at all my jokes and stories about Dad, which is always a bonus! I was there for a couple of hours and had a great time. When Jean took the girls up to bed, I had a chance to talk to Dad about the cancer. I explained that I was fine, I wasn't worried and that I wouldn't know any more until after the appointment with the consultant on Thursday. By the time I left I felt, well, pissed, but apart from that I felt very encouraged for the future, and pretty lucky. The reason for this was the girls. Both of the girls were great fun, with lots of stories and dreams for the future. Do you remember your childhood dreams – what you wanted to be? Someone once said: "The only difference between dreams and goals is the willingness to work toward them!" Who said that? Oh yeah! It was me.

Apart from being really enthusiastic, the other thing that made me feel humbled in their presence was their strength of character. You see Kirsty is diabetic. She is little more than a baby and yet she has to undergo daily hardship, and always has the threat of a bad attack around the corner. And this is something that she will have to live with for the rest of her life, like millions of others. Does she care? Does she moan about it? Does she look for sympathy? No is the simple answer. Not only is she incredibly brave, as I'm sure all children with this and other serious conditions are, but she pushes herself all the time to succeed. Kirsty is on all sorts of teams for dance and gymnastics, and is knocking on the door of the national squad. I was encouraged. If a child can go through that sort of illness every day, how hard can having 'arse cancer' be? So on that positive thought I went home to see how Rachel was holding up and also to try and get some sleep.

CHAPTER 7: CANCER: THE EARLY YEARS (Days really)

I had mentioned to the guys at my office that I would probably be a bit late for work the next day. I arrived at the office once the morning meeting was over, around midday. It is a strange thing being told that you have cancer. Although you are officially ill, you don't have anything to show for it. Apart from a slight hangover, I was no more physically ill than the day before. In order to convince people that you are ill you really need some visual evidence; coughing, sweating, arm in a sling or a plaster cast would be really good. However, because I had none of these things, interacting with people was a little disconcerting, though mainly for the other person I have to admit. They don't have anything to focus their attention on, no cast to write on or tissues to offer you. It's a bit of a non-event, and no one wants to ask you how you feel because that's a pretty daft question in their minds, even if you are OK, as I was.

So I sat down with a couple of the people closest to me and told them what I knew, which to be honest wasn't that much. I had cancer, it was not good and I had no idea what was going to happen until after the appointment next day, Thursday 24th. One of my main concerns was what I was going to do work wise. Obviously if I did die it wouldn't be a major problem; however as I was convinced that I wasn't going to "shuffle off this mortal coil" just yet, I needed to start thinking about my short-term future. What was I going to do with the company? How was I going to survive financially, self-employed with no sick pay? Oh, and the little matter of having to move house within the next fortnight although I hadn't found a flat yet – and moving isn't the cheapest or easiest thing to do in London at the best of times. "It never rains … ' is an understatement, but 'c'est la vie.'

For my next trip to the hospital Rachel asked if she could come along. Whilst I didn't really want anyone with me I understood that it was important for her – to feel that she was contributing and was there for me. That was never in doubt. I don't think there is a nicer, more considerate person in the world – far too nice for me by a country mile. On reflection I must admit that it is a good thing to have someone with you for any important meetings and appointments. We grabbed a taxi up to the hospital, made our way to the relevant reception and waited.

The book I was reading, *Shannara*, was going well and I found it an excellent outlet for my mind to wander, and forget about the present situation. As mentioned, it is a fantasy novel, and I had dived in feet first. As a child I had never really been a great reader; I'm still not a bookworm by any means, although moving to London changed the amount I read considerably. Not only did the move increase my workload and stress levels, but also it meant I had to deal with public transport. For those who don't live in London there is an unwritten rule that you are not allowed to speak on the Underground, and God forbid smiling or laughing, and making eye contact is nearly a shooting offence. People will look at you as if you have just grown a second head if you engage in idle chitchat! Reading is the only option.

I digress; sorry it happens! So we waited, read some more, and were eventually called. As I couldn't think of any news worse than I had already been given at the last appointment, Rachel came straight in with me. I was, however, wrong on the bad news front. Entering the room I shook hands with Alex and Dr Ballinger and was introduced to the consultant surgeon, Mr Lunnis. He was an extremely friendly guy, and made Rachel and myself feel more relaxed almost immediately. We started with some small talk, went through my personal details again, asked how I was – that sort of thing. I would recommend having a definite idea of what needs to be achieved when entering into any meeting, let alone one that could feasibly be the most important one of your life. On orders from Mum, I had a list of things I wanted to know; things she wanted to know to be more exact. First off was this whole cancer thing. I didn't really know why I had it, although a decade or so of fairly unhealthy living was my guess. The medical standpoint on what causes cancer of the large bowel is that they don't really know, although diet is now being linked to the onset of colonic cancer. I asked if it was my "fast living, womanising, heavy drinking ways", with a fake southern American accent and a wry smile.

"We are not completely sure," was the answer.

"Not sure? OK, what about my smoking? Did it cause the cancer because I can't remember sticking any ciggies up my butt! And should I give up?" Mr Lunnis looked over at Alex and Dr Ballinger for help.

This was not the sort of conversation he was used to having with people who had just been told that they have cancer. They shrugged; I smiled and explained that I was aware of the seriousness of the situation but I wanted to get on to the *what is the cause and what can we do about it* part. I have a tendency to reduce everything to a business decision type mentality. Here was a problem just like any other; I wanted to eliminate the cause and start to set some goals to achieve a successful outcome. This is not how everyone does things, I appreciate that, but it was the easiest way for me to deal with the situation. I wanted to feel some level of control in the fairly uncontrollable emotional roller coaster type position I found myself in. Mr Lunnis understood and we got down to business.

"The preferred method of dealing with cancer of the colon and rectum is surgery" explained Mr Lunnis.

"Ok."

"Fifty years ago," he explained, "a surgical technique was developed called an Abdomino-Perineal Excision of the rectum." I raised an eyebrow at him; this was no time for big words. I looked over at Rachel and gave her little reassuring thumbs up; fifty years ago, no problem, I thought. He continued: "It is a fairly major operation which is designed to completely remove the threat of cancer from the region."

"Sounds good," I agreed. "So what does the procedure involve?" I was feeling pretty optimistic: *completely remove the threat of cancer – cool.* Mr Lunnis then went on to explain the whole operation to Rachel and myself:

"An incision is made from around your diaphragm all the way down to the base of your stomach," he explained whilst trailing a finger down my front to just below my beltline for added effect. "Once you are opened up we will go in through your stomach, take out your insides to get to the large bowel – obviously, they will be replaced after the procedure is completed. Then we shall remove your entire large bowel and your anus, w ... "

"What do you mean by *remove my anus*?" I felt that this little titbit needed further investigation.

"Well it is like an apple core. To be on the safe side we feel that it would be advisable to remove all possible areas where the cancer might spread to. So the large bowel and the anus are removed and where your anus was we would simply sew it together." He reiterated, with a twisting hand action to emphasise the apple core motion, just in case I had not got it completely the first time.

"Ok, so this was fifty years ago – what new fangled operation have we got now?" I knew that I was on to a loser here, but one can try.

"I'm afraid that is it. There are other complications that you should be aware of though."

"Such as?"

"Going in through the stomach does bring us into close proximity to your genital region, and there is a chance of infertility."

"That should return to normal however!" chipped in Dr Ballinger.

"Indeed," agreed Mr Lunnis. "However there is another potential problem in that area. Running from your genitals up towards your stomach are a couple of nerves that control your erection. The surgery will be very close to these nerves and there is a chance that they might be damaged, which would therefore lead to permanent impotency."

"What sort of chance?" I enquired.

"About 30%: 1 in 3."

"You've never been in sales have you?"

"Err, no!"

"Don't give up the day job: that was the worst pitch I've ever heard!"

"I'll bear that in mind."

"So you're telling me that although in the last fifty years we've sent men to the moon, invented the Internet, and developed computers that can fit on the head of a needle, the best you can offer me is to remove my sodding arse?"

"Well yes. If we are to be certain that we get all of the cancer I can only recommend this procedure."

"But what about the Sunday papers – I can't very well read them standing next to the toilet can I? It's just not the same!" I had gone on one, by this stage. Remove my arse! Sod that for a game of marbles

"You *would* have a colostomy bag, however, which is admittedly not the same but it is not as bad as you might imagine!" commented Dr Ballinger.

I just looked at her. It has been mentioned to me that I have what my girlfriend calls my Paddington Bear stare when I'm annoyed. And at that precise moment I was annoyed. This was not the kind of back-up plan I was expecting. A stoma or colostomy bag? I don't think so. I appreciate that there are thousands of people who live full and rewarding lives after they have had a bag fitted. Frankly at that moment I did not give a shit. "I am a working professional!" I reminded the good doctors. "I have to interview people all of the time. What is going to happen if say I fart in the middle of an interview? Will my shirt just puff out?" I said whilst plucking at the base of my shirt in order to imitate the effect of a blast of air from just left of my belly button. "How am I going to explain that? 'Oh sorry – just farted!'" That elicited a small punch in the kidneys from Rachel who was behind me. I looked round and was confronted with that very female of stares which basically says *behave or you're on the couch.* "OK. So what would happen if I did nothing at all?" I asked.

"The tumour would continue to grow, and eventually it would kill you!" said Mr Lunnis.

"How long would I have if I did nothing?"

"About twelve to eighteen months!"

"So what you are saying is that I have about twelve months to live then, should I do nothing?" I clarified.

"Yes," said Mr Lunnis.

"Go on, could you say it then. I've always wanted someone to tell me that I had only twelve months to live." Don't ask. It's just that well I'd already done the *You have cancer Mr Davies*, thing and I felt that this finished the set in a Machiavellian sort of way. This resulted in another kidney shot from the missus.

"Ok. You have twelve months to live!" obliged Mr Lunnis.

"Thanks. I still don't understand why I would have to have the whole lot removed!"

It is easier if I just explain this part without all the science getting in the way. Firstly, whilst surgery is the most common treatment, the full-blown Abdomino thingy what-cha-ma call-it isn't the only operation. Every cancer has different qualities, and therefore variations of treatments will be applied. Each doctor will also take into consideration individual factors such as age, general health, and the type and size of the tumour, and whether it has spread beyond the bowel. From the images developed from the CT scan, there was concern that the cancer might have spread into the lymph nodes, which is not good. Aside from that heartening thought, the positioning of the tumour itself was problematic. Allow me to explain. Imagine that the colon/bowel is a hosepipe. In a lot of cases the tumour can be removed by simply cutting out the affected area, and then the two open ends of the hose can be joined back together. Just to be awkward my tumour had decided to grow further toward the (continuing the analogy) tap end. Meaning that there would not be enough of the pipe to re-attach at both ends. It was closer to the rectum or sphincter muscle than would allow a simple chop and patch job. Obviously both Rachel and I chuckled at the mere mention of sphincter, as it was the first time we had heard it in a non-*Wayne's World* type situation.

"Why can't we nuke it or something?" I urged.

"Due to your age we would be concerned about the long-term effects of an aggressive chemotherapy or radiotherapy regime," said Alex.

"The effects of this sort of treatment might have serious ramifications for you in later life, say in twenty years' time. As you are so young we would advise against this sort of action!" she continued.

"I don't care, I'm not going to have my arse removed just like that!" I was not a happy bunny as you could imagine. "Look, three days ago I had an ulcer and now I've discovered that I've got cancer and that you want to remove my arse-hole, right?"

"Yes," replied the doctors in unison.

"So what makes you think that I would care about problems that may or may not occur in twenty years' time? I don't give a monkey's about what might happen in a couple of decades' time. I want some other options!"

"That is obviously your choice Mr Davies; however this is the only course of action that we could recommend", explained Dr Lunnis. A bag! It might sound vain but I was just not into it at all. I had an image of me running down a beach doing my David Hasselhoff, with this see-through "bum bag" that was permanently attached to my waistline flapping around. Bollocks, I thought. "There have to be other options. I want another opinion; there have to be other treatments available!" Mr Lunnis said that he was due to have a meeting with some other surgeons within the next week, and that he would mention my case and see if they were aware of any other procedures that might be applicable to my situation. I thanked them all, apologised for getting ratty and was just standing to leave with Rachel in tow when I was stopped.

"Before you go, I'd just like to personally check the position of the tumour." Dr Lunnis said. You are having a giraffe mate, I thought.

"Excuse me?" I actually said.

"I'd like to check your back passage myself so that I can get a better idea of its size and positioning." I just looked at Dr Ballinger, then back to Mr Lunnis and simply shook my head.

"Do I have a choice?" I enquired.

"Of course," both of the doctors said. However I didn't really believe them.

"Through there?" I said pointing at the door that I'd been through on my first visit.

"Yes please; if you could just go through, drop your trousers and hop onto the bed we will be through in a mo."

"It's not like *Mr Ben!*" I exclaimed. "He goes through the door and gets to be a cowboy or spaceman. I go through a door and get fingers shoved up my arse; it's just not the same," I muttered under my breath whilst walking into the examination room, wishing that the shopkeeper would simply appear and whisk me away. Just for good measure not only did Mr Lunnis do the single digit disco dance up the old back passage, Dr Ballinger also had a play. Although this was not my idea of a fun Thursday afternoon, all joking aside both the doctors and Alex were unbelievably supportive and helpful, and I will never really be able to thank them and all of the staff at Homerton Hospital enough. If this is the state of the NHS I thought, then it is nowhere near as bad as we are led to believe.

Ten minutes later, with the aid of Rachel, I walked, a bit like a cowboy, out of the hospital. Rachel was obviously concerned but knows me well enough to wait until I'd calmed down a bit before discussing all of the issues that had just arisen. In order for that to happen we made a beeline for the Living Rooms, and then The Hogshead, which, I'd recently discovered, was now serving something called a Stella Tower – Game On! We had a lot to discuss, and did so throughout the evening. I thought that I was handling it really well. In the last forty-eight hours I had gone from thinking that at worst I had an ulcer, to not only finding out that I had cancer at the age of thirty-one, but having to face the possibility that I could lose my arse as well, to which I was quite attached. It's hard to really put into words what goes through your mind, and everyone will react in a different way. Me, well, I was not going to take this sitting down. Perching gingerly would be a better description. My mind had found its corner and was playing Twister by itself. So I did what any self-respecting male would do – got drunk and completely ignored the situation. So we talked about other stuff. Whenever I was left alone for a moment and my mind tried to make a break for it, I would simply read my fantasy novel. Even if Rachel just went to the toilet I would read. It was like a defence mechanism, to ignore reality and submerge myself in another world of wizards and demons (bit of a geek I know, but I was having a weird week), with not a back passage invasion to be had anywhere. Some may say that it is unhealthy to do this. That it is just a form of denial, and they would be right. I had no doubts that I would have to deal with the situation but at that time beer and a bit of escapism seemed to be my emotional crutch and I was OK with that. I reported in to Mum and Dad over the phone then, rang work and told them that I was not going to be in for the next couple of days and set about getting well and truly *Jo Banana-ed*. So we drank, I read, Rachel talked, and then we went home for a proper smoke. This was no time to be conscious.

CHAPTER 8: THE QUEST BEGINS

A lot of people I talk to say things like *I couldn't imagine what I'd do if that happened to me*, or *you're really brave for the way that you're dealing with it*. I was not brave at all. In fact if I look back now I would say I was churlish and to a certain degree selfish. I almost took the revelation as a joke. I buried my head in the fantasy books that I was reading at the time in order to escape the seriousness of the situation, therefore putting undue pressure on my family and friends. I told everyone that I had cancer, in a way adhering to that old adage, "a problem shared ... ." Whilst my friends and family would no doubt object to this reflection, I do feel that I should have kept it to myself more so as not to further upset those who were close to me. Hindsight is a wonderful thing, but what is done is done. Whatever the news, however you initially deal with it, going to the pub might not be the way forward for everyone. It will reach the stage where you will get on with it, and moping around will not change the fact that when you eventually wake up to the problem *you will* still have cancer.

Owing to the bad news about my lack of apparent options in dealing with the tumour I didn't want to wait too long to get myself motivated. Subconsciously I was aware that dealing with the cancer, the operation, and having to move house all at once, was not a mentally healthy thing to do. So without sounding corny I went with a one-day-at-a-time approach. I set small goals through the next six months, dealing with things as and when they came along. This might seem a bit daft but it worked for me.

My concerns about the major operation were taken on board by the medical staff at Homerton hospital, and I received a phone call within a couple of days to arrange a meeting with the Oncologist (person who deals with chemo and radiotherapy) on Tuesday 29th July. I spent the next few days keeping busy looking for somewhere to live as I was moving out on 6th August. One of the hardest issues that I needed to address was to ring my brother, Ben, who was twenty-nine at the time, and speak to him for the first time since the news. Telling loved ones was harder for me emotionally than being told that I had cancer. To find out that my brother had cancer would have killed me, so I knew that Ben was not going to take it well. When he first heard from my mum, he did not really get to grips with the situation and, a few days on, I felt it was time to get him sorted and try to put his mind at rest.

This might seem a little harsh, but as with everything that happens in my life, there was more going on behind the backdrop of cancer. He had just accepted a job teaching English in Jakarta, Indonesia, teaching English; and would be away for twelve months from 5th August – just a couple of weeks' time. This was no time for a breakdown or to question going away. I should explain my relationship with *Our Ben*. I have worked from the age of fourteen, always wanted to be the one to get promoted, always looking to 'Make a Million' by the age of forty. Ben has always been more of a self-actualisation person, more into saving the world than taking it over.

Our personal drivers are not the only area in which we are poles apart. A couple of generations back our ancestors were a mix of German and Italian. Although we are the same height we are quite different in appearance. Whilst Ben is slim, blonde with blue eyes, very Aryan, I got the hairy back and the ability to make pasta. That apart, I love him to death. He is without doubt one of the funniest people I know, the writer in the family. Very creative, his emails from his travels around Australia and Indonesia were beautiful and thought-provoking. Someone should give him a job as a travel writer. He is my conscience, the Yin to my Yang, the Cheech to my Chong. Talking to him was going to be hard but he had to go away to teach and that was that. I had to try to convince him that I was serious when I said that I was fine, that I knew that I was going to be fine, to stop being a pussy and go to Jakarta. I promised that I would be up north before he left, for his going away family BBQ on the 3rd August. Having talked to Mum we had agreed that the celebration should go ahead because it was his going away bash and my situation should in no way detract from his pending success. So Ben and myself parted with the deeply emotional words: *"Look it has taken me twenty-nine years to get rid of you. I didn't get you a computer and help pay for your teaching course just for you to bottle it because I've got a dodgy arse. Think of all the money I'll save with you being 10,000 miles away. So stop being a shandy drinking Wendy and I'll see you next Saturday!* This is brother talk for: Good luck, God bless, Go play!

Tuesday came around and once again I found myself in another waiting room. This time and for the rest of my treatment I was alone. I felt it was time for me to take responsibility for the situation I had found myself in. Help would still be offered and accepted, but I needed to feel that I was playing my part, and removing the stress of someone having to be at hospital with me was the least I could do. This time I would be more prepared and had expectations of what I wanted in terms of information. Over the previous week the Internet had been battered by my mum looking for anything that I could be doing to improve my diet, what supplements would be useful to my situation, as well as "real life" hints and tips from web pages posted on the subject. This was how my mum was dealing with the whole cancer issue. Education equals motivation, as

I used to tell the guys who worked for my company. The irony that I was avoiding all that sort of thing I found amusing. What I didn't find amusing was some of the utter crap that is available on the Internet. Throughout the book you will find some of the more useful dietary supplements that I used but I recommend not taking anything without first consulting your doctor. Some of the obvious and more extreme suggestions were to give up:

- All alcohol, smoking, caffeine, the pill, HRT
- Sugar, salt, preservatives, dried/smoked meats, crisps and snack foods
- All dairy products
- All refined and processed foods
- All fried food, all fats and oils, except olive oil
- All red meats and farmed fish
- Your mobile phones, cordless phone, take the TV out of the bedroom and don't sleep between lights – don't ask.

So basically you're being told to go and live on a small island and eat grass. Be careful! There are official sites like Cancer Backup or Bowel Cancer UK that have far better and more realistic information. It is enough to say that you shouldn't believe everything you read. From my point of view one of the issues that needed to be addressed was that of smoking. I'd made my mind up to quit. I failed. Saying that I would try again, and again.

Armed with all this and more information I waited for over two hours in the waiting room before I was called, and I have to admit to being a tad pissed off. The Oncologist was not there for the meeting, so I had to deal with a junior aid to the Oncologist. This really annoyed me; not because she was bad at her job – it was that she wasn't able to answer specific questions about my situation. What information she did have was a list of upcoming appointments that I needed to attend. The initial CT scan showed that there were anomalies within my lymphatic fluid; this and my insistence that I did not want the big op had encouraged the team to recommend a course of chemo and radiotherapy. Now, you know how we expect to wait an age for appointments with the NHS? Well this was not the case with my upcoming schedule.

My first visit would be to the Fertility Clinic at The Royal Hospital of St Bartholomew, also known as Barts, on the 4th, 6th and 8th of August. Chemo and radiotherapy would have a detrimental effect upon my sperm – Jaffa Time – but I was assured that my little fishes would be fine after the treatment. On 13th August I had to be back at Barts for my radiotherapy planning. I didn't really know what that was, but how bad could it be? I was also scheduled for something called a *Peripherally Inserted Central Venous Catheter* to be fitted, which is abbreviated to a PICC line. This I didn't like the sound of, but I knew that a catheter was just a small tap that is inserted into your vein so I wasn't *too* worried. Next it was Chemo time. This took the form of two weekends of continuous chemo feed, starting with Friday 15th August and then Friday 29th August. Once that little session was over I would receive a 5-week block of treatment, lasting from Friday 5th September to Monday 13th October, which comprised two weeks of radiotherapy, the first and last weeks of the block, with three weeks of chemo in between.

This, I was assured, was quite an aggressive course of treatment that hopefully would aid in dissipating the tumour. Once I'd been told all this and given all of the relevant information on the treatments, the junior doctor decided that it was time for her to investigate the tumour manually. I did not even know this girl. I had waited over two hours to not be seen by the right doctor, only to be told that the Oncologist, who wasn't anywhere to be found, would answer my questions at a later date. Then after being about as much help as a chocolate teapot, she wanted to stick her fingers up my arse. I was not a happy camper. "Why don't we get the cleaner in or maybe the receptionist to examine my arse?" I exploded. Once again I found myself on yet another table on my left side with legs up by my chest.

"Is this some type of secret handshake, like they have in the Masons?" I asked. "Except everyone has to stick digits where they are not supposed to be." The young doctor just smiled reassuringly. "Tell you what though," I added, "I'm never going to accidentally insert any part of me in the wrong place again when I'm with a girl." I stammered as she dug deeper. Have you ever watched or read James Herriot – *All Creatures Great and Small*? Enough said!

"You know that old chestnut – Oops wrong hole!" This brought about a small gasp, followed by a laugh and the withdrawal of hostilities. She knew, she'd been there and was sympathetic. With a knowing glint in her eyes she asked me to replace my trousers and come back through to the main room. I'd talked her down, like a hostage negotiator saving my under siege arse.

Although I had managed a small personal victory, I was still extremely unhappy about the fact that I had wasted several hours on not seeing the right person, not getting the answers I had wanted and once again being invaded by any ol' Tom, Dick and Harriet. So I went to console myself with another few chapters of my book – oh and another Stella Tower. When Rachel arrived at the pub I bitched like a little girl, and passed on all of the information on my upcoming treatments to her, so at least one of us would remember the finer points in the morning.

"How bad could it be anyway?" I said in a several pints of Stella later fashion.

"I can cope, no problemo!" I announced. Rachel nodded in a sage like manner, and prepared herself because she knew that I wouldn't.

NB: To all the men reading this: Wwhilst it is accepted that at no time should we ask for directions or read the instruction leaflets of anything (because we can fix it anyway!) it must be advised that upon receiving instructions on upcoming treatments DO read them all. I didn't, and whilst my video works really well this was not much use to me in hospital, and I had several shocks over the next few months owing to lack of preparation. You have been warned.

CHAPTER 9: FAMILY: PRESENT and FUTURE

An old Samurai saying states: "*A decision should be made within seven breaths in order for the Samurai to be successful in their endeavour!*" Or something like that.

Once I had made the decision to not give up my arse without a struggle, I found that everyone had an opinion on the subject. The strange thing was that this turned out to be an almost exact 50/50 split. Pretty much all of the males agreed that I should fight for my right to read on the toilet, whilst most of the females thought that I should go with the doctors' first assessment and not risk further endangering my life and the possibility of side- effects from radio- and chemotherapy, which could still be manifesting themselves for up to twenty years. Why was this so? Whilst it is only my opinion, I think it is down to how we view problems and ways that they need to be rectified. I don't know if men are more prone to playing the odds, but unless it was 100% certain that I would die, there was always a chance. Most of the women that I spoke to would rather be certain that they would be OK than take the risk. This is of course the more sensible approach but that's why it's great that men and women are different; it would be really boring otherwise.

What has this got to do with the price of fish I hear you ask! Well, not much really I have to admit. However, eventually you will have to live or die with any and all decisions that you make. This is true in life and is especially pertinent if you find yourself in this sort if situation. On the plus side any decision is better than not acting at all because if you do nothing *you will* die.

So once you've chosen your path, live with it and don't regret what you have chosen because that is just counterproductive. I had chosen to fight and therefore I had to live with the consequences;

whatever the upcoming treatment dished out I felt that I would be ready, and as for saving my arse, well something would come up. In retrospect it seems funny that I was so convinced that I could cope, or would be ready for the next few months. If I had known what was to come I doubt that I would have been as confident. Luckily I was blissfully ignorant of what was to come and therefore I just pottered around like I didn't have a care in the world. No matter how confident you are, however, certain realities need to be addressed. With the upcoming family BBQ in mind I rang both my mum and dad and asked to speak to them both before the party about what should happen should it all go Pete Tong. We needed to discuss my will.

Rachel and I travelled up from London on the Friday night. The pre-party meeting with my parents was scheduled for the Saturday afternoon. It was going to be a scorcher all weekend; the summer of 2003 turned out to be a record breaker. Although my parents had only been married for about a quarter of my life, it was important for me personally that it was just my mum and dad to whom I talked, not my step-parents. Dad came round and after lunch we went through to the lounge to "chat". Now I had never really thought about having a will, primarily because I did not actually have anything to leave behind, give or take the odd debt. It was quite a surreal situation.

My parents were sat next to each other on the couch, with myself on a chair just opposite. Nothing came to mind to say. I'm sure a lot of you reading this will have a will drawn up already, especially if property or children are involved and obviously if you are married. You must be wondering what the big deal is. The only thing that I can say is that the will and discussing it with my parents was not the issue: it was the fact that we were *discussing* the will with the very real threat that it might be used sooner rather than later. In all honesty I think this was the first time I had taken my situation seriously. I had spent the last couple of years running my own small sales and marketing company (franchise is probably a better word) and I had managed to do quite well for myself without, however, having anything much to show for it. Hindsight is a wonderful thing. When I had money in the bank I was advised to save and invest it in new offices, which obviously enlarges the head organisation without any risk on their part.

So after the crappy last six months that I had just endured, all I had to show from the previous six years of work and sacrifice was a minor heart attack, a tumour up me bum, and some interesting footwear. Not really the legacy I was hoping for. We discussed the situation and my resistance to having the big op. I was still positive that it was the right thing for me, and that something would come up. So the job of dividing my impressive estate had started. All that I had to leave behind was an impressive video and DVD collection – Rachel gets those and pretty much anything else she wants; Ben gets the Zippo which I have had since I was eighteen plus several pairs of boots. Mum requested the cowboy boots because I've pretty much been wearing them since I was fifteen (not the same pair obviously) and it is what a lot of my family and friends associate me with. Dad also gets a pair. And that was all I had.

It wasn't what I had envisaged. Honestly, I did not know what I was expecting to happen. The thing is that when you are younger you think that you can take on the world, that you create your own destiny. In some cases that is true, but for the majority of the time I felt like a twig in a universal game of Poo sticks, being hurried down a storm-swollen raging river with little control and having to get on with things as they happen. This can be viewed negatively, as I had done in the past, or you simply get used to the unpredictability of life and just hang on and enjoy the ride however long that ride may last.

What would happen at my funeral is something that I had thought about. I don't know if it's just me, but I had an image in my mind of what it would be like. Things like who would be there, lots of friends, etc. Problem was I had to admit that I did not have many friends or people who would give a shit whether I was around or not. This is not really a complaint more of a realisation that I had not really lived my life in a way that would have a positive impact. Those whom I would class as my friends are the greatest people I've met, and I wished that I would have the chance to spend a lot more time with them and my family. One thing I had a view on was the music that would be played; I thought that the Pink Floyd classic "Wish You Were Here" would be the song for me. The words *we're just two lost souls swimming in a fishbowl year after year*, seemed to be scarily prophetic in terms of the way the majority of us live our lives; apathy about what's going on and living with an *it's not my problem* ideology. Plus I liked the irony with the title and the song's proposed use. It is funny what you think of when you are in the presence of the Reaper. Well maybe not the presence yet, but I had received the invite. With that over and done with, my parents and I went for a well-earned drink.

The BBQ was a success. The main reason why I feel that I was so confident that it wasn't my time to die was the example set to me by my grandparents and the support of those close to me. My nana at this time was ninety-two and still the strong woman she always had been. My granddad was eighty-five and still had the sense of humour that got him through the war and through cancer of the stomach at the age of eighty.

How could I be worried with genes like that? As well as my grandparents being there, we had a full house. My aunty and uncle had come over from Liverpool; also there were some of my brother's friends, our joint friend Rob, Janet and Ian from across the road, and of course both full sets of parents. I managed to spend time with everyone alone without disrupting the party. But, saying that, it takes a lot more than a spot of Poop-Shoot problems to get in the way of a decent party with my lot, which is one of the reasons I love them.

With the party over, Rachel and I went back to London and I prepared for the start of the treatment. First stop would be the Fertility Clinic for a bit of Bag and Tag. Monday morning was the first of my three visits to the Fertility Clinic at Barts Hospital. This was the part of the treatment I felt that I could really get to grips with, although I hadn't spanked the monkey three times in five days since being a student. I felt confident I would persevere, and rise to the occasion. I was ushered into a waiting room, and had to fill in a load of forms about what to do with all my Mark-cicles in the future. Once the paperwork was completed I was led through to another smaller room that was bare apart from a rather worn chair and a coffee table full of relevant literature for the job at hand. The nurse handed me a clear beaker. I resisted the urge to ask her if she felt like giving me a hand, locked the door and made myself comfortable.

Fifteen minutes later I surfaced, and made my way to the lab. I gave my sample to the doctor, apologised for the delay citing that it was difficult to perform under pressure and that I needed a ciggie and left. I had to return on Wednesday and on Friday by which time I felt I was getting the hang of it. On the Wednesday I had to move house. It also happened to be the hottest day of the year so far at 98.8 degrees.

Moving house at the best of times is complete and utter ball ache; with the stress of the past few weeks and my dedication to preserving the Davies gene pool it turned out to be an absolute nightmare. Rachel and I finished at two in the morning, having once got lost in deepest darkest southeast London, and having to make four trips in the van to cart all our stuff from the old place to the new. Not recommended whilst being treated for cancer I can assure you – where are your mates when you need them hey?

CHAPTER 10: THE SUN AND THE MOON

Having spent the weekend with the family I found that I was even more determined to beat this cancer thing, and consequently my mental state improved even further. I had not been worried by the cancer up until this point and had a renewed sense of purpose. It was time to concentrate on getting the rest of me into the best physical situation possible, and it was not going to be easy. As I mentioned earlier I had received a lot of information pertaining to cancer in general as well as colonic cancer specifically via Mum and the Internet. Whilst I have to admit that some of the information was very helpful a lot of the Internet stuff was bordering on the lunatic.

However, I was acutely aware that I was not what you would call a prime physical specimen, and as one of the side-effects of the chemo treatment is the reduction of white blood cells which aid staving off illness and infection, I had to mend my ways and quickly. I left my parents armed with a shopping bag full of vitamins and supplements that according to my mum would aid in the fight against the cancer as well as the side-effects of the treatment. As I mentioned previously, it's best not to take anything until your doctor has checked it but some of the suggestions are pretty obvious.

As always it is best to give up smoking; it always surprises me how many people continue to smoke when faced with cancer, especially outside of the cancer wards – take the hint! I had stopped smoking cigarettes by now – third attempt – and was only occasionally having the odd "herbal" ciggie mainly because it did help with getting some sleep. I had not been having more than three to four hours sleep a night for the past twelve months, but I do not as a rule like to take addictive drugs like sleeping tablets. Rest is something that you will need a lot of if you're going to get through the treatment. I also decreased my alcohol intake and type of alcohol consumed. This aided with the giving up of smoking, as I am still tempted to have the odd ciggie when having a drink. Stella was now a rare treat and I only occasionally had the odd glass of red wine as it is supposed to be better for you – something about being higher in antioxidants from the red grapes' skin and seeds (this dietary information however seems to change on a daily basis so, as with everything, excess is not gonna help).

My diet had to change; I am quite a good cook but was woefully lazy in the kitchen and have several take-away numbers actually programmed into my phone, which is not a good sign. As for vitamins, well, fruit and veg now inhabited my new flat. Previously I had considered extra salad on my kebab was the healthy option. I would suggest extra vitamin C and supplements to increase your intake of antioxidants. *Note: Do not take vitamin C during Chemo. This is actually quite important – you will discover why.* The more that you help yourself the better the outcome will be. You want to be in the best physical position to fight off any germs whilst receiving treatment. I found that a lot of what was happening during this part of my treatment was beyond my control, so I was eager to take advantage of any opportunity that might hopefully have a positive effect on my situation. I found that the mere feeling of being able to have even the slightest effect upon my situation was just as important to my mental well-being as it was to my physical condition.

Every cancer is unique and correspondingly so is the treatment regime. And owing to my requesting alternative solutions to the "smash and grab" attempt on my arse that had been initially recommended, I had been sent details of my personal chemo and radiography timetable from Dr Lunnis et al. This was, however, all about to change because that's the way of things. "He who dares, Rodney" to quote Del-Boy. Let me explain. A couple of days after the BBQ my mum had a visitor at her work. Mum worked at a Further Education College called Burton Manor and an old friend of hers named Penny Moon popped in. It was the first time in nearly a year that they had met and obviously had quite a bit of catching up to do, and my situation was brought up. Penny had known my mum for years, and had met me before when I was about sixteen. Penny had worked as an educational psychologist back then, and had an interest in astrology (as you do) and had been asked to speak with me when I was younger. Apparently I had a problem with school. I prefer to think that it had a problem with me – anyway I digress. Now, out of the blue she turned up at my mum's work. When my mum rang me she was very excited.

Penny apparently had a good friend who was an oncologist. He was based at the Clatterbridge Centre of Oncology on the Wirral and worked with a surgeon at the Royal Liverpool Hospital's Linda McCartney Centre. On top of this spooky bit of coincidence the oncologist and the surgeon he worked with specialised in – wait for it – colonic and rectal cancers! *No Way? Way!* There is more! Not only had Penny Moon just popped in out of the blue; ignore the coincidence of her knowing an oncologist who happens to work twenty miles from my parents' house in Chester and try to see past the fact that both he and his surgical partner specialise in the exact area that I was afflicted by. Note instead that he was also the only person in the country who used a special form of radiotherapy that is applied directly to the tumour, which could enable the surgeon to try an alternative procedure, which would negate the need to remove my arse.

I was stunned; then she told me his name – Sun Myint, and the first thought that went through my mind was, yeah right! Some old friend called Moon, who thought it would be useful to do a full Astrology Chart reading for me when I was sixteen and having trouble at school, recommends some guy called Sunny, who just happens to be the only person in the whole of the UK to do this treatment! Shame she wasn't called Cher I told my mum over the phone. I was later to be proved thankfully wrong about my initial assumptions, but be honest what would you have thought? You have been getting some, let's say, inconsistent advice from various parties, then you have this situation presented to you. After a while I agreed with my mum that this was too big an opportunity to pass up; irrespective of whether we were successful or not this was the first potential alternative that had presented itself. I asked mum to try and make an appointment for me to see not only Sunny but his surgical partner Dr Hershman as well.

Within three days the first appointment was made for 26th August just in the middle of my first session of chemo. See what I mean by fate playing its hand? It is not the problem that counts; it is the decisions you make when faced with them. I did not know if this was going to be the answer – the doctors might not have been able to operate owing to the tumour's proximity to the muscle tissue of my sphincter. I had a feeling though that this was fate throwing its hat into the ring and I was just going to have to see how far it would take me.

The strange thing about getting this remarkable bit of good fortune was that I was initially reticent about mentioning the news to my current team of Dr Lunnis and Dr Wells (the oncologist). I was worried that my original team would be put out by my getting outside help, and maybe treat me with less than the due care and attention I might have got had I simply gone through with the rear-section operation. As usual I had no real time to think about it; I had just finished having a relationship with a plastic cup and was preparing myself for the upcoming treatment laid out in the chemo/radiotherapy timetable that I had received. (*Note to Fertility Clinic: you have to try to think of a better receptacle than a plastic cup. Not only is it hard to hit it is dangerous ta boot. Trying to get your "old boy"' into a decent firing position without getting it stuck in the cup is not easy. Trust me I know. Why not use a type of freezer bag or something? Just a thought.*) My next appointment was only a couple of days away on 13th August and it was for the radiotherapy planning. I rang Alex at Homerton Hospital and explained the situation about finding a possible second option to the "Big op". She assured me that it was perfectly understandable and that this information would be passed on to Dr Lunnis so he could contact doctors Myint and Hershman. That all sorted I just got on with waiting for the next appointment at Barts for the radiotherapy planning.

The planning was scheduled for late morning on the Wednesday and as per usual I did not have a clue what to expect. The radiotherapy unit at Barts is just a little away from the main building, in a newer section. Newer, however, is not always better especially when the main building is pretty impressive. The main site is hundreds of years old, built primarily of a sheer white stone and the architecture viewed from the main gate is really quite commanding. The best way to explain it is if Inspector Morse was a doctor this is where he would work. I had now begun to get the hang of finding and reporting to receptions in hospitals; having sailed through I settled in for a wait and a wait I got. The waiting room was considerably different to that of a general hospital. By this I mean that in a cancer-based waiting room you know that the people in there are all very ill.

I became acutely aware that I stood out like a sore thumb. I realised two things immediately. Firstly, that I was not that ill at all. Some of the people in that room were seriously ill and I felt a bit guilty that I was so lucky to only have bum cancer. Secondly, that I was about thirty years younger than anyone else in that room, visitors not included. This I found to be quite a sobering situation and it begged the question "What have I done to myself in order to be in this situation?" Whilst I am fully aware that people of all ages get cancer for neither rhyme nor reason, I felt that my situation might well have been self-inflicted and I cannot stress enough that if you are going at it like Sonic the Hedgehog on speed, beware. No sermon: I enjoyed smoking, liked drinking, worked twelve to fourteen hours a day and ate anything that could be nuked for breakfast. 24/7 is all well and good, but you have been warned. Don't go mad – be sensible.

OK sorry, that was a bit of a sermon there, but I was in a radiotherapy waiting room at the age of only thirty-one, and it kind of makes you think!

Anyway back in the waiting room I was busy concentrating on not seeming too young and well when eventually I was called into a small side room and the planning procedure was explained. In essence "planning" is determining the optimum position for the radiation to enter your body – it sounds like so much fun when it's put it like that doesn't it? The form of treatment that is primarily used on this form of cancer is external radiotherapy. The tumour is bombarded by the radiation, which hopefully destroys the cancerous cells. The main downside to this is that healthy cells are also destroyed in the process. The duration of the treatment lasts only for ten to fifteen minutes at a time, and if you are to have several sessions they are administered daily, with a weekend break to allow your normal cells a breather. Each patient will have an individual schedule. Mine, initially, was from the 8th September to 15th October inclusive, which worked out to be about thirty sessions. This might sound daft, but to allay any old wives' tales – you will not become radioactive and start to glow like the "Readybrek kid".

The planning as mentioned was to maximise the effect of the radiotherapy on the tumour. This is done by literally being laid on a table and moving your body around until everything is in place, and then they draw on you. "Okey-dokey then." I mean what are you supposed to say? I was led through to the planning room where I was confronted by three young female radiographers and a physicist, who asked me to slip off my trousers and hop onto the table face down, butt in the air. No problem I thought; now we men are open about the fact that we are easily pleased, and call me old fashioned but I reckon that given the choice eight out of ten male arse owners, who expressed a preference, would rather have their arse stroked and drawn on by three attractive young ladies than Helga the destroyer of Butts! I'm semi-naked and the table was cold, if you know what I mean, and things were going swimmingly. I was beginning to enjoy the fact that my arse had been exposed for several minutes and no one had tried to shove anything up it.

"OK Mr Davies," said one of the team.

"Please, call me Mark." Calm or what!

"OK, Mark. In order to make sure we have the exact area we will have to take a quick X-ray of your lower bowel."

"No problem – where do you want me?" GO-GO eyebrow.

"Oh just stay there." A small smile had started to traverse her face and it wasn't a *Hi, how ya doin?* Smile. It was a, *I know something you don't, smart arse* sort of smile. I recognised the glint and knew something was amiss.

"To make sure that we get the correct position of the tumour we need to pass a liquid that will show on our X-ray into your back passage."

"I thought it was going too well," I sighed

"Oh come on now, Mark; it won't be too bad, and will only take a couple of minutes," said the lead radiographer.

"That's Mr Davies," I said with a smile. I'd had worse than liquid up the old poop shoot I assured her as the three of them left the room ready for the X-ray. It still concerns me that if X-rays are so safe, why does everybody flee? Once I'd been X-rayed they returned and set about finalising the treatment parameters. Once complete they made three small tattoos around my lower regions in order for the radiography team to replicate the exact position of my tumour during my treatment. Two of the tattoos were drawn on each of my upper thighs. The third was positioned in line with the others, just at the top of my builder's cleavage – I think that sounds nicer than butt crack! Forty-five minutes later I was done and out of there, no worse for wear. Next stop, the Pagett Ward and my PICC Line in two days' time on Friday morning.

Friday arrived and I made my way back to Barts main buildings in order to receive my PICC line. There are several ways that chemotherapy can be administered and the treatment again will be designed for each individual's situation. Apart from intravenously receiving the chemo, it could be administered in tablet form, injection into a muscle, injection under the skin, and injection into the fluid around the spine, the ever-faithful injection into body cavities or even a cream for cancer of the skin. I made my way up to Pagett Ward and started my wait. This was the first real time that I had been exposed to the debilitating effects that cancer and chemo can inflict. The ward was relatively small and was split into two sections. I was led to the back of the right-hand section and informed of the wait. The ward was pretty full both with those people who suffer from cancer and their friends and families. A lot of the patients seemed to be there for the entire day receiving treatment and would obviously require support. I just made myself comfy at the back of the room along with several others who looked at me as if I didn't really belong there.

The majority of the actual patients were sat in a circle, a large proportion of them wearing night attire and dressing gowns. Some had lost, or were in the process of losing, their hair and all of them had a tall metal stand holding their individual bags of treatment. This was obviously the inner sanctum and I was dubious as to whether I qualified as ill enough to join them. Only time would tell. As my mind wandered a nurse approached me and took my name and the names of my specialist team. Nurse is not her correct title; Junior Sister Jane was in her mid to late twenties, 5"4' with brown hair and from up north. This motivated me quite a lot because this meant that I felt like I had an ally, which is of course absurd because they treat everyone the same, but you hold on to little things like that at times such as these.

Straight away we got on really well and Jane explained that it was her job to look after me for the day and that she would be the one to attach the PICC line. Now there are three ways to have chemo delivered intravenously. The PICC line obviously, as well as what is called a Central Line (which I was assured did not mean that it never worked and if it did it would only be with severe delays – London joke) which is inserted through the skin of the chest into a vein near the heart; and a cannula, which is simply a small tube inserted into a vein on the back of the hand or arm. This small tube in the back of the hand was in all honesty what I thought I would be having and I was once again wrong (didn't read the instruction leaflet did I – Doh!).

Jane explained to me what the PICC line really was and how it was fitted. I was more than a little shocked I can tell you. In essence, as opposed to the small catheter or cannula which I was expecting, this was a more serious business altogether. She explained to me that a small tube would need to be inserted into a major artery near the heart. The line is inserted at the crook of your arm and is pushed through your vein until it reaches its desired position near your heart. "You are having a giraffe!" I said in my calmest possible voice. Before all this could happen I would have to undergo an X-ray and several blood tests, so I made myself comfy and proceeded to read my book.

During the course of the morning I rushed about from one building to another dropping off blood samples and being X-rayed, until finally I was told that I was ready to have the line fitted. Jane was to fit the line and took me through to a closed-off section of the ward in order to begin. She showed me the line, which was about as thick as a cocktail stick or a straw from one of those cheap juice drinks. It was going into the crook of my left arm and would be pushed up through my vein until it reached a position just above my heart. Now apparently you can have a local anaesthetic. I didn't. The whole thing should not take more than about twenty to thirty minutes. I lay back on the bed and proffered my left arm, which was placed on a pillow in order to support it properly.
"What I'm going to do first is find a suitable vein and then insert a catheter through which the PICC line will be threaded," Jane stated. "I would

suggest that you don't look as it can sometimes be a bit messy," she continued.

"Cool," I said, and proceeded to look. The choice of which arm you would prefer to have the line affixed to is yours, I would suggest the opposite one to which you usually favour, and as I was right-handed I went for the left arm. It is quite important as this line might be in for up to six months (dependent on treatment) and you will have to shower and work with this in situ.

Sometimes there may well be the odd hiccup, and as it is me there was one. Whilst trying to thread the line through the vein it collapsed – the vein that is not the line. Blood spurted out like a bloody fountain from a cherub in dire need of a slash!

"Don't look," squealed Jane as she tried to stem the gushing.

"What, why? Cool! Looks like when Vivian chopped off his finger in the *Young Ones*." I exclaimed. "What happened?" I asked.

"The vein collapsed so I'll have to find another one," said Jane apologetically.

"No worries" I said. "Fill ya boots – I have lots of them!" A few minutes later it was all done.

"That was quick," I said

"I'm just going to draw off some blood to make sure that it works properly and then we will secure it to your arm," informed Jane. The blood was drawn and all was good. The line itself looked weird sticking out from my arm, and the hole where it entered my skin was quite apparent. The line ran for about ten centimetres out of my arm and it was this that had to be secured so that it wouldn't get caught on something and be pulled out.

The two major potential problems with the PICC and the Central Line are blockage and infection. I had to report to the unit twice a week in order to see if these problems were arising. The line is to be flushed out at least once a week with saline to avoid blockage Jane informed me. The line was secured using large clear plasters which meant that it was still visible but clear from infection. Whilst the line itself was not really a problem or hurt at all once it was in, living with a tube in your arm will require some degree of common sense. I was instructed to keep it as clear from infection as possible and under no circumstances should I get it too wet – no swimming for example. This led to the whole shower/bath problem, which is the same one you would have should you ever have your arm in a cast following a break.

"So a Tesco bag then," I enquired.

"No need. We have something even better," explained Jane. "We have a special bag which is designed to keep everything nice and dry." A couple of minutes later she returned with a small bag with something in it, and handed it over to me.

"Pour moi? You shouldn't have!" Ignoring my crap French accent Jane explained how it was to be used and mentioned that it would be invaluable since I was to receive my chemo via an infusion pump (a small bottle type thing that would be attached to the PICC line), and that I would be able to go home with the pump attached.

This was the first that I had heard about the details of my treatment even though I had already been drawn on and impaled, so I urged Jane to impart a bit more info seeing as I was due to start my treatment in two days' time. All that she had to tell me at this time was the delivery method, i.e. infusion pump, and the type of chemo, which was called 5-Fluoroacil or 5FU for short. However Jane did find some handouts for me that explained the PICC line and its care instructions and further information on 5FU and its side- effects. The shower bag looked like a large bread bag with an elasticised end, which had an extra band of material with Velcro ends which would be wound around the top end of the bag up by my bicep to seal it off. It was going to take me a while to get used to it but I had a feeling that this was going to be one of the more minor things I was going to have to deal with over the ensuing months.

Before leaving I had to have another X-ray to ensure that the line was situated properly within my chest – nice! With this but final task completed and armed with all this useful information (which I forgot to read but luckily for me Rachel did so at least one of us was prepared) and with my shiny new PICC line in place, I bid my farewells and left for the day, with the knowledge that I would be returning in forty-eight hours for the start of the treatment proper!

The thing with the early stages of cancer, as I have already mentioned, is that you don't look any worse for wear. Having this blue tube running from my wrist externally down to the crook of my left arm at which point it entered the skin, all of which being visible through the clear plasters; and then continuing within my body until it reached a spot somewhere near my heart, was all to much for me to keep to myself. I had to show someone my arm; I was literally bursting with excitement. Part of the reason for this was that I had heard from a reliable source that there was a rumour going round work that I was actually lying about being ill, that I was making up this cancer story just to stop me doing any field sales. Whilst my mum found this to be quite unbelievable, I merely thought it rather sad though not wholly unexpected. I had my suspicions as to who the main perpetrator of this rather sick rumour was, although they would of course deny it. Although I had stopped taking a wage from my company, I had still been into the office most days and would continue to do so for as long as physically possible.

The likely reason for this misconception about my health was that I was not prepared to mope around and feel sorry for myself. I tried to be as upbeat and positive as possible about the situation. To be honest I had found that since receiving the news that I had cancer I was actually happier than beforehand. The nature of my business was field-sales-based with individuals driving money through their own sales and by developing a sales team of their own. Once an individual had a team that was big enough to be profitable as a small concern of their own, they would be backed to open a satellite office of their own. Like I'd done with the team that I had sent to Glasgow. The problem is that whilst you get some support from the parent company, you have to use them as sole suppliers of your goods to sell.

Whilst we were running out of product options in Glasgow and I was forced to close it down; my team in London had suffered as well. I had started to rebuild London but with my news and the work that I would have had to put into growth again, I had decided not to worry about trying to save the business and instructed my accountants to start closing it down. I also found that I was far more relaxed about everyday things like the Tube trains being late or missing a bus. I had found myself smiling, yes I kid you not – someone in London, not pissed or on drugs, smiling at people. It was like I had been looking at life through pinholes in a piece of card with all the wrong things being important and taking up too much of my focus and attention. Well, now the card had been removed and, without sounding like a right sad case, the sun was sunnier and the leaves were greener and now I was off to work to show off the new tube in my arm to once and for all put the pettiness of my kind of business behind me. It was good to feel that for once I was in full control of my life. I was not in control of my death, obviously, but I didn't dwell on that bit too much. Even the person or persons who doubted my illness would have to admit the insertion of a tube into my arm would be a tad extreme just to pull a couple of weeks' sick leave, for which I wasn't being paid anyway. Some people – I tell ya!

Everyone dealt with my illness in his or her own way. Some were in denial, some could not bring themselves to talk about it and were very upset, and some followed my lead and were positive and upbeat about the situation. I have to admit that I quite enjoyed seeing the faces of those doubters upon viewing my new plastic appendage. My former housemate and friend Jon, who is as hard as nails, couldn't deal with the whole – well hole – thing, and went to find a quiet corner to think happy thoughts. The greatest effect, although I wasn't instantly aware, was on Rachel. She later confessed to me that this was the first real time that the severity of the situation had hit home. Whilst I was quite pleased with the tube in my arm, this was the first physical evidence of my illness, and let's be honest a bright blue tube isn't that subtle. Some people with whom I did not have the greatest of personal relationships with did surprise me with their genuine concern, most notably the joint CEOs of my part of the organisation. I can't thank Jez and Steve enough for their help and support throughout those next several rather taxing months: guys it was most appreciated.

With my Barnum's Freak Show over with I decided to call it a day and head home. It is amazing how tiring being positive and upbeat is when you have just spent four to six hours in hospital waiting to be impaled. Upon leaving work that day, having worked with some of these people for five to six years, I knew that I would not be going back once I was well. I knew the people who would continue to be close to me, and those who where purely interested in what financial benefit I had provided in the past. This was quite a sad realisation; people who I thought were friends were in fact no more than colleagues. This may well be the case for other people as well as myself. I found that the people who I knew fell into three distinct categories: those who were actively with me all of the way; those who cared very much but just could not deal with the situation on a day-to-day basis, but were still going to be there once the worst was over; and those who simply paid lip-service, said the right things, made all the right supportive noises when I was actually there but at the end of the day didn't give a shit. The advantage of this is that once you are well again (and a successful novelist) you will know who your real friends are; and those who need to be told where to go, maybe even drawn a quick map just to make sure … Well you get the point.

That's my bitch over with, but I was upset because I like to think that I make an effort with everyone. Anyway I had the little matter of chemotherapy to be getting on with on Friday and that was going to be an adventure because I knew virtually nothing about what was going to happen, although I had been assured that my hair would not fall out, hopefully, and that the first session would only be for the weekend.

CHAPTER 11: MAKE MINE "TO GO"

As far as I knew chemotherapy happened in hospital. You went for the day, got plugged into the drip and either stayed in as an in-patient, or went home at the end of the day returning in two to three weeks for another session. I was asked if I wanted to be an in-patient for the initial two sessions of the treatment or have the takeaway version. Whilst the hospitals and the staff had been above reproach, I did not feel like sitting around for days on end feeling sorry for myself in hospital, taking a bed from someone who was really ill. Even with my new line I still did not feel that I qualified as ill yet. So for want of a better phrase I had mine to go. Before going into how to attach a bottle of chemo to your arm it is time for a bit more science. Sorry!

What is chemotherapy? If you accept that cancer is simply a case of cells multiplying far too quickly and then buggering off around the lymphatic system to cause more damage, chemotherapy is the use of anti-cancer drugs (cytotoxic) to destroy or at least interfere with the ability of those cancer cells to divide and reproduce themselves. It reaches the parts other drugs can't reach, if you like. As with everything to do with cancer, each and every treatment is unique. There are over fifty different types of chemo, some of which are used exclusively and some of which are combined. This has been cleverly called "Combination Chemotherapy". As with radiotherapy this damage is not exclusive to the cancer cells, hence the side-effects, but the healthy cells can normally repair the damage whilst the cancer cells cannot.

My particular chemo was called **Fluorouracil (5FU)** and it had its own range of side- effects:

* **Mouth sores and ulcers**

- **Diarrhoea**
- **Gritty eyes and blurred vision**
- **Skin changes such as darkening**
- **Temporary reduction in bone marrow function – this is the moody one with anaemia, risk of bruising or bleeding and infection but will not generally occur until seven days after the treatment, getting worse towards the two week stage and returning to normal after twenty-one days. The extent to which your blood count drops will obviously depend upon the strength of the treatment, although this is checked regularly to monitor how well your bone marrow is working.**

Less common side-effects for my treatment are:

- **Nausea and vomiting**
- **Hair loss**
- **Changes in nails, i.e. changing colour or going brittle, chipped or ridged**
- **Sensitivity of the skin to sunlight – both during and for several months after treatment has finished (wish I had read that bit before going on holiday)**
- **Rashes**
- **Soreness and redness of the palms of the hands and the soles of the feet (sometimes known as Palmar Plantar syndrome) also known as pretty goddam painful**
- **Increased production of tears (not just when going to the toilet)**
- **Oh, by the way, you will probably be infertile at least for a while as well, hence the bag and tag.**

Apart from that it should be pretty plain sailing so nothing to worry about really! Luckily for me I did not read the handout about all of these side-effects so I strolled in on Friday morning bright and chipper and ready to be dosed. I've since been asked why I did not read any of the leaflets about the treatment and side-effects and my answer was simple. Why would I want to know that at the end of the week something bad was going to happen? All that would do is to upset me for the entire new week. This way every day would be like an adventure and I would just get on with dealing with what was happening, not what might happen. Whoever said ignorance was bliss was correct in my case. Don't know, can't panic.

I strolled onto Pagett Ward at just gone 9.30 on the Friday morning armed with my book, a bottle of water (very important to drink a silly amount of water during chemo, and, just for good measure, it was also turning out to be one of the hottest summers on record) and my shiny new tube in my arm. I stood at the front of the ward waiting to be noticed. Then I sort of leant on a nearby table and waited to be noticed followed by sitting on the table waiting to be noticed. That worked.

"Can I help?" a passing observant nurse enquired.

"Ah yes, sorry (why I was sorry I have no idea – must be an English thing), mmm I'm here to see Jane, err, for my chemo," I added. I'd hate them to think I was there just to pick up nurses.

"Got my PICC line and everything," I explained proudly showing my left arm.

"No problem. Just go and take a seat over there at the back and I'll let her know that you are here. What's your name?"

"Davies, Mark Davies," I stammered. There must be something about being at the doctors or in hospital that turns normally articulate people into useless monosyllabic fools.

"Ah yes there you are, up here on the board. Just pop over there and she'll be with you in a bit." A little tick was placed next to my name on the day's schedule board and I was officially in. I passed by the inner sanctum of hardcore chemo patients and seated myself quietly at the back.

Looking back, a cancer ward might not be the place to start up idle conversations with all and sundry, but when I'm nervous I can't help myself. I managed to last for only about five minutes before getting the urge to talk to someone, then it was the full-on "so what ya in for?" making the place sound like a hairdressers – "bit of a perm! You?" I knocked that on the head after a while and decided to return to my book seeing as most of the people did not want to engage in witty dialogue.

Then out of the blue Jane appeared like a traffic warden thirty seconds after your ticket runs out (except a lot nicer, obviously) to relieve my boredom. I was asked to follow Jane to the inner sanctum and took my place with the rest of the patients who were already plugged in. It sort of reminded me of those dodgy horror movies where they capture people and drain off their life force for some evil escapade. Once I sat down I again felt really uncomfortable – well not really, but definitely out of place.

The circle of patients was primarily made up of older people, a lot of whom were in-patients and were dressed in nightclothes. It was all very white and grey like some Eastern European *film noir*. Until *I* arrived that is; jeans and cowboy boots might not have been the standard chemo attire but it is difficult to know what will go with a blue tube in your arm and a portable chemo dispenser. First there was the obligatory blood test, then the itinerary for the day. As my chemo was going to be a portable version, the doctors had to make sure that it was completely attuned to my body before sending me off for the weekend. "So can I have one of those medicine stands then?" I asked Jane.

"Why?" Jane looked puzzled. I have to admit that it might have seemed like a bit of a strange request but you always see them in *Casualty/ Holby City* etc. and it definitely means that you are officially ill. I explained this to Jane and just got a resigned shaking of her head. "You will have one in a minute. You have to have a vitamin solution before we give you a chemo booster which will drain into your system before we attach your 5FU."

"Cool!" Like I understood what she was talking about.

Jane went off to deal with some normal people whilst I waited for my stand to arrive, with an inane grin on my face. Looking around the circle I realised that the whole conversation was probably heard by the rest of the patients and had elicited several curious stares. After a short while Jane returned with the stand, a drip bag containing the first solution to be administered hung from its top. The bag was attached to my PICC line via a long drip tube and with that done I was advised that the drip would take about an hour and that I should just sit back and relax.

Now I don't know about you but I was a bit of a fan of the *Carry On* films, and having my own drip stand was really quite exciting. So I went for a walk with my stand – had to! The stands wheelbase was obviously designed by the same people who developed the shopping trolley. So whilst it primarily went in the right direction, it did have the annoying habit of periodically shooting off at mad tangents for no reason at all. After a while I was bored of shooting around the corridors although I was coerced into performing an impromptu mini pole dance for a couple of elderly ladies (who looked quite pleased with the attention, and even gave me a little ripple of applause) and returned to my seat.

After what seemed like an eternity it was time for me to be "plugged in" to the 5FU infusion pump. I didn't have a clue what to expect and was pretty surprised by the pump itself. The only thing that I could compare it to would be a Lucozade Sport bottle with a meter of clear tubing attached to the top. I gave Jane an incredulous look as she proudly presented me with this "bottle" and attached the end of the pump's tubing to my PICC line.

"What am I supposed to do with this?" I asked, examining the inflated balloon that filled the inside of the bottle.

"The balloon inside holds the chemo and will administer the treatment continuously over the weekend, so that by the time you return on Monday it will have delivered the correct amount and hopefully will have completely deflated."

I raised an eyebrow: "But what am I supposed to do with this – the bottle? How in God's name am I going to carry it around or get to sleep?"

Jane smiled. "Ah I see. Well, we have this carry pouch which the pump fits into and can attach to your belt." The carry pouch was produced and it was obvious that the same style guru who brought us such designer classics as *Hospital Smock* or *Prison Inmate Jump Suit* designed it. It was basically a weird little *Bum Bag*, which was attached to a natty blue belt with 100% real plastic clips – Oooo! I hear you cry! Indeed! There was nothing that I could do about the situation, and I told myself that maybe the fashion implications were probably not at the forefront of the design spec considering it was for holding chemotherapy. So I folded the tube which ran from my arm to the pump, folded it back on itself, so that it would run down the inside of my sleeve and out of the bottom of my shirt. At the very least, I didn't have to walk round London with tubes sticking out of me. Thus fixed, I made my way home.

CHAPTER 12: REALITY STRIKES

Later that night Rachel returned from work and took the whole bottle thing really well. Neither of us really understood what the infusion pump entailed; so this little bottle, whilst being stylishly challenged, wasn't as bad as we might have imagined. Saying that, sleeping with it dangling from my left arm was a completely different kettle of fish. With the bottle full it weighed about the same as a full bottle of Lucozade, so my major concern was that should the bottle fall out of bed, or I turned over during the night, the weight could pull PICC line out of my arm. Jokingly I suggested that if I turned over too quickly the bottle could come flying over my shoulder and clobber Rachel while she slept. Whilst that might be quite amusing, from my point of view anyway, it would have implications, i.e. couch time for me!

This might not seem like a major problem, and you might be asking yourself "how can he be more worried about the functionality of the pump than the chemotherapy?" Living with the cancer means just that. I tried to limit the disruption that all of this would have upon my everyday life. Things were going to get worse, a lot worse, so if I were to struggle with the little things, the major medical problems would be a complete nightmare. Not only that, sleep was going to be an important part of my recuperation. This was not going to be the only chemo I was going too receive, so if I could get the little things right at the start I wouldn't have to worry about them when bits of me started to drop off. Bottom line was that I probably got about three to four hours sleep, max, that night, and most of that was after Rachel had got up for work on the Saturday morning.

I finally got out of bed owing primarily to the cacophony that was emanating from outside my flat. I went to the window only to discover that the neighbouring block had become a building site complete with heavy machinery and pneumatic drills all set for an 8 am start. This was on top of the fact that I had moved into the flat in a bit of a rush, and was not aware the road facing the flat had heavy traffic 24/7. This meant that although we were having the hottest summer in recent history I could not open the windows without being drowned, not only in noise but carbon monoxide. Turning away from my window shaking my head with a feeling of resignation, I started toward my bathroom, caught sight of myself in the full-length wardrobe mirror, and just stopped in my tracks. My reflection wearing only boxers is not the best at any time, but this was different. I HAVE CANCER! I think that this was the first time that I really accepted the situation. The image of me standing there with a blue tube running down the inside of my left arm, with nearly a yard of extra tubing running in front of my body, to the infusion pump which I held in my right hand hit me hard. It was bound to happen: I knew that it had to happen; it was just a bit of a shock when it finally did, a reality check in the most poignant way. Whilst my life did not exactly flash before my eyes, certain realities about the way that I had led my life and, more importantly, how I had treated people, did. I had, for want of a better description, a Nick Hornby "Hi-Fidelity" moment. I thought about my ex-girlfriends and how I might have been nicer to say the least; about my current relationship with Rachel; about life in general and what it might have in store for me now.

I just stood there looking at, but not really seeing myself, in the mirror. It was like one of those mid-morning stares where you zone out, but with meaning and without the drool! Then from the edge of my consciousness I started to hear the radio as life began to take focus again around me. I heard a haunting introduction to a tune that I did not recognise and was drawn into the song, hearing every word with crystal clarity. Emotionally, I was not at my best, reflecting on past mistakes and life in general, and hearing "White Flag" by Dido for the first time – well this was the proverbial last straw. I just sat back onto the edge of my bed and sobbed. Well not quite sobbed, but I definitely had "quibbly bottom lip" in a major way, which for me is sobbing. It was a quality song and in the state I was in I felt that she was singing about me; and the whole *not giving up* I transferred to my current medical situation. I don't know for how long I sat there, but I eventually decided to get up and move on.

I am not the sort of person to dwell on things and so decided that it would be best to file this emotional moment in a corner of my mind so that it would not affect both my mental and physical fight against the cancer. I would have to deal with both my past and my future at some stage but my priority at this moment was the present and trying to beat the illness, and the best way for me to do that was to stay focused and positive. My immediate goal was to reach the other end of this cancer thing, arse intact, and then I would have time to address any other issues. I got up and left my room vowing to buy Dido's new album so that I could play "White Flag" whenever I wanted, as opposed to it randomly creeping up on me, and turning me into a dribbling wreck.

CHAPTER 13: LET IT BE ...

The rest of that first chemo session over the weekend was much of a muchness. The effects of the treatment are not immediate so it was all about the bottle and not what was in it. On the Monday morning, I went back to Pagett Ward to have the bottle removed and my dressings changed before heading off to work. This is really an easy way to have your chemo administered; it was literally a case of having the adjoining tube removed from the PICC line and then rinsing it though with a saline solution. Changing the dressings was far more traumatic. I like to think, like most men, that I have a fairly good tolerance for pain but there is a reason why men don't wax.

All Jane had to do was to remove the large plasters that kept my PICC line clean and free from infection; but hairy arms are not the best things in this situation. I was a big girl's blouse to say the least. I moaned, I complained, and it hurt more than putting the PICC line in. The problem was not just the fact that the plasters where pulling out my arm hairs, slowly, but the realisation that I would have to have this done to my poor little arms at least twice a week for the next eight to ten weeks. "Let me do it myself," I pleaded, but to no effect. New plasters were affixed, I thanked the girls and left for work, having to return towards the end of the week in order for some more arm hairs to be liberated from their follicles.

As you might have guessed by now, my mental approach to the cancer situation was to just relax and go with the flow. I believe that it was stress that partly contributed to the development of the cancer in the first place, so stressing after the fact seemed pointless. The human body however does not always listen to the mind and mine was beginning to display signs that it was not happy with the current situation. One of these signs was the development of strange sort of target like, itchy, discolourations on my hands. I had suffered with this once in the past when I was dealing with some business crisis of one type or another, so I was not worried about them reappearing. However, with a healthy dose of chemo thrown into the equation I thought that it was best to mention the marks and an appointment was made with a Doctor Cerio who was a skin specialist at the North London Hospital in Whitechapel East London.

Again, fair play to the NHS, I found myself in the doctors' waiting room the very next day. Finally, I was admitted and to my surprise found that I had attracted a crowd. Not only had the good Dr Cerio made time to see me, my oncologist had appeared along with two other interns. The conversation was pretty standard; I amused myself – the doctors couldn't work out if I was joking or in need of psychiatric intervention. Eventually a very long name, which I am not even going to try to repeat, was given to the target thingies and a suitable cream was prescribed. Dr Cerio was really quite excited by the whole affair, owing to the relative rareness of the sores, and insisted that I not only had an ongoing open appointment at the hospital should they return, but that before I could leave the hospital I had to go to the medical photo lab to have my hands photographed for posterity. So there you have it; it was clearly going to be one of those days. My hands are forever captured on film somewhere in east London; to quote Richard Littlejohn: "You couldn't make it up."

Upon leaving the hospital, I popped into my office to check in on Rachel and then left to go and meet up with my dad and step mum Jean who were down again for the day visiting three thousand-year-old mummies at the British Museum near Russell Square. So a quick tube to Euston Square Station, followed by a brisk ten minute walk down the road, and I was at the museum. Living in London is a bit like working at McDonald's: I don't just mean sweaty, smelly, stressful and repetitive, which it is a lot of the time – I mean that when I worked at McD's the last thing I wanted to eat was a burger. I live in one of the most vibrant and culturally diverse cities on the planet and this was the first time I had been to that or any museum since I had moved to the *big smoke*. It was, for want of a better term, pretty fucking impressive. I won't go into details but I have since made more of an effort to do some of the tourist stuff that Londoners themselves seem to ignore.

Feeling as if I had achieved something for the day, I joined Dad and Jean for a drink at a local little café/bar. Continuing with my theme of trying to improve my body's chances of staving off further infection, I declined alcohol and went for a pint of freshly squeezed orange juice; cultural and healthy, will the new and improved Marky D please come on down! It was nice to see my dad again so soon after the BBQ, because as mentioned over the last decade contact had primarily been a couple of hours at Christmas. My mum had mentioned he had taken the news of my cancer probably worse than anyone else had. Why this is so I do not know, but I have my own personal views on the situation and suffice to say that when people say, "It is never too late to make up", it can be! After half an hour or so they had to get off, so I popped to the loo and noticed a slight rumble in my stomach, though I couldn't work out why. We went our separate ways; they went back to Chester and I started to walk the half mile or so back to Euston Square.

Gravity: the force that attracts a body towards the centre of the earth or towards any other physical body having mass. I assume that like me you probably have never given gravity much thought. Unless you are falling out of a tenth storey window, you probably never will. It seems, however, that gravity also works within the body. As soon as I started walking, the initial disquiet that I had felt in my stomach prior to leaving the café became considerably less, well, quiet. I started to try to increase my walking pace hoping that I would make it home without having to make a poo stop.

I had walked no more than a couple of hundred yards before the first eruptions started. Oh shit, I thought, this is not going to be good, as my arse let rip again. My mind started to race – what am I going to do? What has set this off? Although I have not mentioned it, my initial symptoms – extra toilet time etc. – had not gone away during all this time so I was accustomed to being prepared to bolt for the loo at the drop of a hat or fart, as was often the case. This was different, however, and I could not work out why.

Then it hit me: the pure orange juice. Remember I mentioned that vitamin C was not a good idea whilst receiving chemo? This was obviously why. So there I was with a bad case of "Oh my God I'm going to shit myself." The walking quicker was not working. The human body has a sick sense of humour. Whilst running would bring my arse to a nice safe toilet quicker, the more speed that I attempted the more the contents of my stomach wanted too be free. Mind over matter – that was the key. I concentrated, on my breathing, on the direction that would take me to the station as quickly as possible, and most importantly (anyone who has had a bad dose of "deli belly" on holiday will understand the next bit all too well) on trying to distinguish between a fart and possible development of "turtle heads".

Sweat was pouring down my face as I turned the corner into Euston Road. I was hit by a painful stomach cramp that made me acutely aware that a major gas eruption was imminent! I had to try to hold it in; it might be the fart too far; this might be the one to break free; the one to follow through; and I would not let that happen. I clenched my butt cheeks together for all they were worth, but gas is, by its very nature, adept at finding its way through small cracks. I was resigned to my fate, but if I could let it out slowly, a little at a time, I might be able to save my pants. So I produced a nineteen step, walking fart. You know the type I mean – every time your foot hits the ground for some reason a little of the fart escapes. It reminded me of the yard scene in *The Great Escape* where the allied prisoners distribute the soil from the tunnels out of holes in their trouser pockets onto the ground. Eh! Oh! Oops! Aftershock! That will need a hot wash! Wasn't ready for that one I chuckled to myself. To my dismay the station did not have a toilet and I felt that the time was at hand; my waters hadn't quite broken in the literal sense, but whatever was in my gut was most definitely alive and wanted out, pronto! I dashed back up the station stairs and frantically looked around for inspiration. Nothing. I had to find a loo, any loo, and now. I made my way around the corner and spotted some small hotels. I entered the first one that had open doors, and tried to still myself. I made for the reception to plead for the use of their facilities, with my "I have colon cancer and *I will* shit in your reception" trump card ready, should I have a problem.

By this stage, in order to keep everything where it should be, I was no longer walking but sort of lumbering. My legs were only moving from the knee down which were pressed as tight together as possible and the look of distress on my face must have been evident because although the receptionist did not really speak English he recognised that it must be an emergency and pointed towards a set of glass doors. I am sure I saw a smirk on his face as I lolloped towards salvation. I was through the doors and down the hall desperately looking for that familiar little silhouette of a man (Scaramouch Scaramouch can you do the fandango?)

on a door. The belt was already undone as I barged through the toilet door and into the cubicle. In one flowing movement, I had turned, dropped pants and closed the door just in time for … OH MY GOD! I very nearly lifted off the seat. This was not natural; this kind of destructive force could only be man-made. I pressed my palms against the cubicle walls for support; this was not good at all. Every time I thought it was over and made a move to stand and leave, that little fiend gravity would be there to stop me. I was in there for ages.

Eventually I overcame my fears and made my way out of the cubicle, tried to freshen myself up as best as possible in the mirror and left for home. I sort of smiled at the receptionist as I gingerly strode past with as much dignity as I could muster. He looked at me shaking his head and half laughed as he turned away. I knew I would have the last laugh though – that toilet didn't need cleaning: it needed exorcising. It took me in the region of an hour and a half to get back to Surrey Quays from Euston Square. Normally this would only take about twenty to thirty minutes. This was primarily due to emergency poo stops at Liverpool Street station, the McDonald's down the road from Whitechapel Station and the Wetherspoons just by my flat. I wasn't even going to make the 400 yards to home without a stop it seemed.

By the time I collapsed through my flat door, I was dehydrated and felt that my insides had been squeezed empty much like a sachet of ketchup over your fries. No more vitamin C for me I thought as I disrobed and clambered into the shower, before falling asleep on the couch. In life we all have a tendency to repeat our own mistakes or those of our parents etc. Not in Chemo World! I never even looked at vitamin C for the rest of my treatment; even the fruit and veg section at Tesco would give me the willies and send me darting for the loo. The moral to this story is to avoid vitamin C at all costs whilst receiving chemotherapy. Although citrus fruits are a no-no I lived on bananas, grapes and health shakes for breakfast during this treatment. I have also been told that pineapple juice is good.

Before my next session of chemo, which was a fortnight away, I had an initial consultation with Dr Myint and his surgical partner Dr Hershman at the Linda McCartney Centre (LMC) on 26th August in Liverpool. This was to discuss my situation, whether I would qualify for the treatment, and assess if their ground breaking procedures could go some way to saving my arse. They had requested a copy of my original CT scan, which I retrieved from Homerton, and made my way up to Chester. I truly believe that a large part of my attitude towards my having cancer and the way that I took everything with a smile was due to my Liverpudlian heritage. This opinion was further cemented by some of the conversations that I had on the London to Liverpool train.

If you have never been to Liverpool, it is a place where people will take you as you are, and not let a little thing like adversity get between them and having a laugh. A prime example was when on the train I got chatting to this guy in his fifties and eventually we got round to why I was heading up north. Having not had cancer for very long I still had not quite got the hang of talking about it. It was not just that I was new to the cancer thing but the fact that, and this may sound strange, I was a little embarrassed about what sort of cancer I had. At the time I didn't know that colon or bowel cancer was the second biggest killer cancer in the UK – I'd never really heard much about it. As far as I was concerned I had cancer of the arse, and that's just not that cool! So I just said that I was heading up to go to the doctors, but wanting to talk is another scouse trait.

"Is it serious?" said my train companion.

"Well quite serious, but nothing to worry about really."

"Well that's good. So can't any of these London doctors do something?"

"The doctors in Liverpool might have some alternatives that I could try. You see … " This was it; I was going to have to tell him.

"You see I'm going to the Linda McCartney centre because I have The Big C."

"Ah Crabs!" he said with a smile on his face, and I just burst out laughing.

"Yeah that pesky seafood hey! Gets everywhere," I said.

I stayed at my mum's in Chester that night and headed over to Liverpool the next morning for an eleven o'clock appointment. The LMC is attached to the main Royal Liverpool Hospital (RLH) and is a fairly new building. My mum accompanied me for the appointment, and we were cautiously optimistic that Doctors Hershman and Myint would be able to help me in my quest to save my arse. We made our way towards the second floor where their joint surgery would be held. I had brought the copy of the CT scan with me so that the doctors could assess the size and position of the tumour. The CT scan was A3 size and I had kept it in its original hospital envelope; whilst taking the lift to the surgery we were joined by a gentleman with an envelope of his own.

"I'll show you mine if you show me yours," I said holding up my CT envelope.

"I think I'll be seeing that soon," he said. "I'm Mr Hershman."

"Oh hi." *Great – of all the people to have a laugh with and it is the one person who could probably end up having a large say in my future.*

"I'm Mark Davies, this is my mum, and I think we are meant to be seeing you and Dr. Myint this morning." Mr Hershman said that he knew who I was by the Homerton Hospital sign on my CT scan and took the scan from me so that he and Dr Myint could evaluate it before they saw me later that morning. Once I had checked in with reception Mum and I made our way through to the waiting area and waited, for ages. After a couple of hours, I was called and led through to a separate examination room with a bed in it. I knew that the bed was not a good sign and more "backdoor" investigations would no doubt be in order. "Oh joy!" I was left alone in this room for what seemed like forever but was probably only five minutes. I don't know if doctors are aware that hospitals and especially examination rooms with telltale examination beds are pretty goddam intimidating places at the best of times, and that to leave someone alone in one of these aforementioned rooms is therefore bordering on psychological cruelty.

Eventually doctors Hershman and Myint entered the room with the nurse who had brought me through originally, Margaret, who was a complete angel throughout my treatment, and probably the only sane one there. After the introductions we got down to the problem at hand.

"I really, really don't want to have to have a bag and my entire arse removed if at all possible," I asserted. "I don't understand why, if the tumour is so accessible, it can't be cut out. I understand that it is close to the muscle but surely we can shrink it. I don't care what I have to go through – nuke me, drug me, do what is needed. Honestly, I don't care if I have to go through six, nine, twelve months of complete agony; as far as I am concerned that is a small price to pay for the ability to sit on the loo."

"Well, that's what we are here to discover," said Mr Hershman. He then went on to explain the procedures he and Dr Myint might be able to use for my situation. I will endeavour to explain the basics because it is important and could possibly save your arse one day too.

There are two procedures involved: one is surgical and deals with the removal of the tumour, which is called Trans Endoscopic Microsurgery (TEM); and the second is a special form of radiotherapy that is called Papillon. Although not widely used in the UK these treatments have been around for more than a decade and are common in several places in Europe. My position was that I could not understand why it was easier to cut me open, remove everything, probably make me infertile, then completely remove my entire colon and arse (talk about fly catching with a bazooka), than to simply popping up the old jacksie and removing the tumour that way. This is the crux of the TEM.

The procedure basically enters via the "bum hole" and using very cool technical stuff they are able to cut around the tumour and staple the hole up (the tumour hole not butt hole), et *voilà*. Obviously this procedure will not work in everyone's case. If the tumour is too far along the colon, too big or too far developed thus threatening to break through the colon wall and bugger off to cause more damage elsewhere this will negate the usefulness of the procedure. The saying "The sun will shine on every dog's arse at least once" came to mind. I was just hoping that my arse was hairy enough to qualify, south-facing and ready for some solar intervention. This type of operation can be undertaken either by itself or in conjunction with Papillon radiotherapy.

Papillon radiotherapy is a method of applying the radiation directly to the affected area, which allows the level to be more focused without damaging all of the surrounding tissue. How they directly administered the treatment was yet to be discussed; however, the name, Papillon, i.e. butterfly, gave me a mental picture of the position that I might end up in, which I was not completely happy with.

"The CT scan that you gave us is not very clear I'm afraid, so we will have to have a closer look ourselves, with a digit examination," said Mr Hershman.

"One digit or two?" I enquired.

"Oh just the one," he laughed, "although we might have to use the sigmoidoscope which has a light inside it for us to have a better look. So could you just ... "

"Pop up onto the bed lying on my left side with my knees up towards my chest?" I ventured. "I know the drill." With the help of Margaret, I was positioned precariously with my bum hanging over the side of the bed. Gloves were donned, lube was applied and contact was made.

"Yep I can feel it quite clearly," said Mr Hershman

"You're not the only one," I squealed,

"Would you like to have a feel?" said Mr Hershman to Dr Myint.

"Not at the same time I hope?"

"Of course not," said Dr Myint as he approached and took over where Mr Hershman had just finished. With that all done I was formally introduced to the sigmoidoscope and I felt compelled to have a word.

"You do realise that it looks like a lightsaber!" I ventured. I am not completely convinced that Dr Myint had seen *Star Wars*. Although Mr Hershman did find this very amusing, it did not dissuade him from impaling me with it. This was not good at all. I had not yet got over the double examination whammy up the back door, and now I had a sodding lightsaber lodged up there. To make it worse the doctors wanted to get the best view and so were moving it around like a games console joystick. Mr Hershman could see through an eyepiece that was attached to the end. After some umm-ing and arr-ing Dr Myint evidently wanted to play. "Can I have a look?" enquired Dr Myint. He really wanted to have as close a look as possible and went for the multi-angle technique with unabated gusto. Either that or he had just encountered the "End of Level Big Boss" hiding a couple of inches up my arse. After some more umm-ing and arr-ing Mr Hershman wanted another look. "What do you think?" he said as he retrieved the protruding joystick.

"Not quite sure yet!"

"What's the problem?" said Mr Hershman

"Look there!"

"Where?"

"There!"

"I can't see the problem!" said Mr Hershman

"Not problems, just, well, look – there!" said Dr Myint rather vaguely.

During the conversation the protruding end of the lightsaber was passed back and forth several times, which meant that the end that was up my end was bouncing off the inside walls of my colon and was giving me some serious stinging ring. Enough was enough. "Ladies, ladies, look at us bickering, squabbling. We never used to be like this!" Margaret burst out laughing. "Are they always like this?" I asked her.

"Like an old married couple!" she said, and she wasn't wrong.

"Well I've seen enough. You?" asked Mr Hershman.

"Yes, I've seen enough as well!" replied Dr Myint.

"Well, can someone take this thing out of my arse then? Ahhhh! Thanks."

"Pull up your trousers and we will be back in a minute," said Mr Hershman. He and Dr Myint turned on their heels and went into the adjacent room to discuss my insides in private, leaving me to clamber off the trolley and fix myself up. I went straight to the loo and tried to release some of the trapped air in my back passage and remove the excess lube.

Having a lightsaber shoved up you bum doesn't half give you the farts I can tell ya!

After a while, they returned and asked if I'd come with anyone. I mentioned that my mum was in reception. She was brought in for their conclusions.

The visual images retrieved from the CT scan had shown some undefined types of "floaty bits" in my lymphatic system but had not been of much help in distinguishing their threat or lack of. So going from mainly what they had both just seen they thought that I had a good chance of qualifying for the operation. This would mean a change in my treatment in London as well as additional MRI and ultrasound scans to see fully the size and depth of the tumour and the nature of the floaty bits. The concern was that the tumour would be a T2-3, which meant that it had not just stayed on the surface of the colon wall (T1 type tumour) but had eaten through the wall and may have gotten into the lymphatic fluids, which is not good.

The doctors did feel that, in conjunction with some Papillon radiotherapy, if the tumour had not spread too far, they might be able to save my arse. Traditionally this type of treatment has only been used on T1 tumours. However, with a combination of traditional treatments, Papillon and the use of the TEM surgical procedure, there are circumstances where a T2 tumour larger than 3cm, might be successfully removed. Uppermost on the doctors minds was the size and development of the tumour and my long-term welfare. Mine however, were far more short-term focussed.

"Cool!" was all I could really manage at that point. With the thank yous all done, and even with the promise of more anal intervention lingering in the air, I left feeling a lot happier, if not a tad tenderer, than I had been only a month previously when I was told that I had no option and my arse was history. I cannot stress enough that whilst I believe doctors will want to give you their best advice and opinion it might not be the best advice for you. *The truth is out there* or up there, in my case. After staying at home for the night and having rung to give Rachel the possibility of good news, I had to return to London, only to come back the following week for an ultrasound scan. This was because I had the next bottle of chemo to put on that Friday, you see, and cancer waits for no man.

CHAPTER 14: BOOTS AN' ALL!

Chemotherapy is not the sort of drug that has an instantaneous effect; it is like drinking Jack Daniels whilst sitting at the bar. You feel fine then try to get up to go to the toilet only to discover that your legs no longer function. Apart from the target lesions (from now on all skin disorders will be called "lergy" because from here on in things start to go wrong and fall off), the only reaction that I suffered after the initial dose was sore gums. Not as bad as I had been led to expect.

"So, any problems?" asked Jane when I returned for chemo part deux.

"Apart from some random lergy and sore gums, no." The plasters were replaced with much bitching and moaning on my part, the second bottle of 5FU was attached and, with a bottle of mouthwash in my possession, which Jane kindly gave me, I left for a weekend of no sleep. And that, as they say, was that.

When I returned to be unplugged on the Monday morning, Jane had some news about a change in my treatment schedule. This was in preparation for the prospective treatment that Doctors Hershman and Myint would hopefully be able to administer. The new treatment schedule was hardcore. I would still receive five weeks of treatment; however, as opposed to the original one week radiotherapy, followed by three weeks of chemo and then a final week of radiotherapy. I would now receive a full five weeks of continual chemo and radiotherapy.

"Weren't buggering around then, were they?" I commented to Jane.

"No! This is quite an aggressive treatment schedule," she agreed. "Don't worry – we'll keep an eye on you," she said reassuringly, as she liberated some more hair from my lower left.

"Ow!"

"Baby!"

With that done, I was off to ring round the various concerned parties to deliver the news of the new and improved nuking program. Then back to Liverpool for the ultrasound.

Whilst all this running around the country was annoying in a time consuming way, the up side was that I could hang out with my family more than I had at any time since leaving home. It was nine in the morning on the 3rd of September and it was Dad's turn to take me to the hospital where the ultrasound awaited. Whenever possible I tried to do the whole doctor thing on my own, and so Dad went to potter around Liverpool for an hour whilst I went into the RLH. The reception of the RLH is cavernous and completely white, almost like the waiting room at the "Pearly Gates" except with added "shell suits". Having been given the relevant directions for the Ultrasound Department by reception, I endeavoured to find my next waiting room. Once seated I had only to wait for a few minutes before a nurse collected me by the arm and started to walk me away from the waiting room and off down some tunnels – well, corridors, but you get the picture.

Usually, being prepared for a new procedure would have been a little disconcerting, but to be honest I was quite looking forward to the ultrasound. Lots of lying around whilst nurses smear goo all over your stomach and "lower regions" then a quick look at the TV and little tiny Davies Junior before we nuke the crap out of it – how bad could it be?

"OK! Mr Davies, could you please go into one of the changing rooms, remove all of your clothes apart from your undies. Leave your footwear on so you don't slip. Oh! And could you use this before returning here," she said gesturing at the seats just nearby and handing me what looked like a white plastic mushroom with an uncomfortably long stem.

"Sure!" I said. "What's this?" holding up the mushroom.

"That is a small enema just to clear you out so that the doctor has a better view when examining you," she replied.

"Knew it – thought it was going too well," I thought. The telltale chimes of doom were gearing themselves up for a big day inside my mind. It was almost as if they knew what was going to happen but thought that it would be more dramatic, or just more amusing, to let me find out for myself.

"How does it ... work?" I enquired, not really wanting to be given an answer.

"I'm sorry – I thought you must have already had one of these."

The way that I was holding the "mushroom" at arm's length as if I was expecting it to go off and the pleading for salvation in my eyes, must have given a hint as to my ignorance. I managed only a shrug and a smile.

"It's very simple; just pop the stem up your back passage and squeeze the cup end until empty. Try to hold the liquid in for as long as possible then just let yourself ... go!" said the nurse.

With that, she left me, a lone figure looking to and from the Demon Mushroom (I renamed it), and the changing room door. I sighed and entered. It was bad enough everyone and their dog had tried to push something where the sun doesn't shine over the past few months, let alone self-abuse. I undressed and found myself in front of the toilet staring at the offending fungi. Just pop it up and squeeze; how bad can it be – it's not very thick! No problem. I sat on the loo and readied myself – pop it up and squeeze – pop it up and squeeze. OK, I can do this. I leant to my left trying to slip my right hand under myself in order to do the nasty! That wasn't working, so I went for the left hand option ... from the front and up? My arse was having none of it. I had no lube so sneaking it in was not an option, and my A-hole had shut up shop; it was like trying to force- feed a child bad-tasting medicine with their lips sealed. Therefore, I used a tried and trusted DIY technique and just forced it in. Although I had already anally sampled several liquids already during my treatment I still found the cold sensation up me bum strange, even when I let the liquid out, which was pretty much as soon as I had got it up there. Then came the cramps and the recognition that my colon wanted to get rid of everything that was up there. As I was nearing the end of the toilet ordeal I started to go through what else the nurse had said to me. Undress, check! Get into hospital gown, spotted! Return to the waiting area outside these doors still wearing your footwear, which is when I spotted my dilemma.

Five minutes, and a couple of pounds and tears shed later, I emerged, gingerly, from the changing rooms wearing only a pale blue gown which came to just above my knees and my cowboy boots! The only person in this part of the waiting area was an elderly gentleman whom I sat opposite. He lifted his head from my boots to my face and I could see the question beginning to form in his mind.

"Hospital gowns hey? Didn't know what would go well with the colour and cut of the gown!" I insisted. His brows began to slowly knit together like clouds colliding under a light breeze, and his mouth looked as if it might speak. "Better than the old ones though; just above the knee – flirty but not tarty I think!" His face had evidentially decided that to talk would have been too much hassle so it again relaxed into its comfortable folds and only a small exhalation emanated from his lips.

To say that I felt daft sitting in hospital with my boots on would be a huge understatement. I felt like an injured extra from *The Dukes of Hazard*. The chimes struck up again as a doctor approached, introduced himself, and sat down next to me to explain what the ultrasound entailed.

The sound of those chimes got louder as I became acutely aware that there would be no soothing goo, only lube, and definitely no nurses caressing my stomach. Holding me down maybe!

" … Then the instrument will be inflated whilst inside you and sound waves will map the interior of your colonic walls. Any questions?"

"Err!"

"Good, follow me!"

I followed him down a small tunnel – definitely a tunnel leading me to my doom, arrgh! Get a grip! Sorry, but I was a bit concerned that my morning of gooey nurses had been replaced with inflations and such like! We entered the examination room and the chimes went *Da Da Derrr*! There was the bed and next to that illuminated by the glow of the monitor a tray of medical instruments, upon which lay what could only be described as a hand-held harpoon gun à la James Bond's Thunderball. *Da da Dada daaa de-na*!

I was ushered towards the bed, assumed the position, and hoped that my butt had relaxed a bit more than before because there was no way that contraption was going to fit. I also noticed as the doctor picked up the harpoon that it had a pipe where the bolt should have been, and that the pipe had what looked like a condom on the end of it. This was the part of the weapon that was to be inserted and inflated whilst being up my bum. I have to admit that the inflation of the condom up me bum was not as painful as the inflation of my actual colon during the Colonoscopy, but just as weird. The procedure was predicted to take up to thirty minutes. However, about twenty minutes into my examination, someone entered the room from the adjacent door.

"Can I help you?" enquired the doctor

"Oh! Err! Sorry der doctor. Just lookin' for da maintenance room like! Ya alright dere mate – sorry bouts dis," he said to me as well as the doctor.

"No problem – it's … " The doctor started to give directions. Now I'm as helpful as the next guy is but there are times and places and this was not one of them.

" … Then left and through the … " continued my oh so helpful doctor/tourist information officer. Apart from the fact that this chap had just wandered in, ignoring the fact that a medical procedure was commencing, and without commenting on the social and psychological effect that this could have had on someone who actually gave a shit, the thing that I most objected to was the fact that the doctor had not removed the harpoon from my arse, and was still holding onto the protruding end. Watch what your hands are doing next time you give directions! Exactly!

Eventually the maintenance guy left and the air powered buggering continued for another five or so minutes. I peeled myself off the bed and made my way back to the changing rooms. Luckily, there were no other patients to see my ashen face as I hobbled carefully out of the examination room. Gratefully I donned my clothes and made my way back through the labyrinth of corridors to the front of the hospital where I rang my dad and encouraged him to come and meet me as opposed to me having to traipse round Liverpool with the demeanour of a neutered dog. A couple of minutes later I was sat in the car on my way back to my mum's for some R&R before going back to London the next day as I had my five weeks of chemo and radiotherapy to start on that Friday. It's just go, go, go this whole cancer thing, I tell ya!

CHAPTER 15: PAPA'S GOT A BRAND NEW BAG

The date was Friday the 5th of September, just over six weeks since that fateful day in July when the bottom quite literally fell out of my little part of the world. It was time to receive exactly what I had asked for in my quest to save my arse - a full dose of chemo. The two weekend sessions had been successfully negotiated and apart from the odd lergy outbreak, being unable to clean my teeth for the last few days owing to ulcers, cold sores and bleeding gums, and my hands feeling a little warm and tingly, my side-effects had been relatively mild. I was fully aware, however, that this next phase of my treatment was going to be different. For the next five weeks, finishing on the 15th of October, I would be receiving the chemotherapy continuously, 24/7.

This was something that would require a bit more planning and preparation on my part as opposed to my wait and see approach. Unfortunately, I found that no one was sure how bad the side-effects were going to be as this treatment was pretty aggressive, but most were in agreement that it might get bad at some point, which was reassuring.

Up until this point, I was still going to the office every day to keep myself busy. I was assured, however, that as the treatment continued I might start to feel progressively more tired and there was also talk of my skin being irritated by the five weeks of radiotherapy that would be starting on the following Monday morning. This meant that although I would have to pop into the hospital Monday to Friday to be nuked every day for the next month or so, I would be spending a lot of time at home. Like most working people, I expected this to be a bit of a culture shock so I planned ahead. While preparing for this extended period of home time I made sure that I had the essentials – Sky TV and an XBOX (with obligatory *Star Wars* game). I also thought that it might be a good idea to have a complete cleaning blitz of my flat – this was in readiness for a severe drop in the efficiency of my immune system mid chemo. I had also stocked up on supplements like Selenium, Echinacea and vitamin E that are supposed to aid with the immune system as well as being antioxidants.

I had been advised to wear loose clothing when lounging around the house owing to possible skin irritation caused by the intensive radiotherapy program that I was about to start. Bearing this in mind I borrowed a sarong that my brother had picked up when travelling through Indonesia a few years previously. I know what you're thinking, but this wasn't a Beckham-esque little Gucci number; it was a dark blue with little white palm trees holiday type sarong. I thought I looked quite fetching in a short, fat, hairy guy in a skirt sort of way! The strange thing was that my primary concern was the mechanics of actually dealing with the chemo bottle itself. How was I going to get around with a tube and hip flask attached? How was I going to sleep? I had secured virtually no sleep when the bottle was attached on the first two occasions, so I was not looking forward to living with it for the next five weeks.

Once I arrived at Pagett Ward I took up my usual place at the back of the room and waited for the day to begin. It was 9.30 in the morning and the ward was already half full. My morning started with blood tests to see how my body was dealing with the chemo I had received so far. That was followed by being plugged in to some type of drip for an hour or so. Eventually it was time to be connected. Jane changed the dressing covering my PICC line, still with much ooing and, moreover, ahhing, on my part.

"Why can't I just shave the side bit of my arm so that the plasters could grab onto my skin and not my rapidly depleting hairs?" I enquired.

"No! You could get an infection and that would not be good!" said Jane.

"But wh … " I was cut off with a look that they must teach at nurse school, that "time to be quiet" look.

"I'll be quiet then." I would address this issue again but now was not the time. Jane went off to fetch my new bottle as I tended to my poor little arm. The first bottle was very much like a Lucozade Sport bottle but this new infuser was a completely different shape. The only things that I could liken it to were either the inside of a roll of kitchen towel or a Christmas size tube of Smarties. The infuser was clear plastic and had what looked like a condom filled with chemo inside. This chemo filled condom was attached to a valve at the end that would feed the chemo into my system via the long tube, which protruded from the end.

"What am I supposed to do with that?" I exclaimed. "How on earth am I supposed to carry that thing around with me for the next five weeks? I can't stick it in my trouser pocket can I? I mean could you imagine the looks I would get; 'Is that a 5FU chemo infuser in your pocket or are you just pleased to see me?' Come on!"

"Not to worry," said Jane. "There is a carry bag just like the last bottle you had. Hang on while I go and get it." With that she shot off to the storeroom to retrieve the carry bag, leaving me to try and work out what to do with this eight-inch (that's a real eight inches not a bloke's eight inches) baton.

"Here you go, it's waterproof and has a belt catch so that you can carry it around easier!" said Jane triumphantly.

"It looks like a large blue willy warmer. You are having a laugh!" I screeched, as I took hold of the bag. To prove the point I put my new little friend into the willy warmer, attached it to my belt and stood up. I had a little saunter round the room, like you would do when you are trying on some new shoes, or in my case chemo filled dark blue willy warmers. I shook my arse, bucked my hips and span round a couple of times and the bottle simply bounced around like an agitated truncheon.

"No, this is not going to work; I feel like a complete dick," I said, turning to see Jane and the entire inner sanctum looking and laughing at me.

"It's fine," smirked Jane. "No one will even notice." More smirking. I undid the belt clip, retrieved the bottle from inside of its multi-purpose portable holder and sat down. I appreciate that looking good should have been the last thing on my mind, but to be honest having cancer was still quite a new experience. On top of that physically I still felt fine. If I had been sitting round in my PJ's at hospital all day it would have been OK, but I wasn't. Not only that, I was thirty-one not seventy-one. I was making a concerted effort to try and continue with my everyday life as much as possible, for as long as possible and therefore, from my point of view at least, it was a concern.

It was time for some lateral thinking. What I needed was a space-efficient way of carrying the bottle and the half a yard of tubing, that would allow me to still wear my suit and not have to be worrying about catching it or the tubing.

"Have you got any tubigrip?" I asked.

"Yes. Why?" enquired Jane.

"I have a cunning plan." I answered in my best Black Adder voice and raised my left eyebrow for extra conspiratorial effect.

"What size do you want?"

"I need it to be as long as my forearm, and quite wide width-ways if that's at all possible." Jane brought over a roll of tubigrip and cut it to size, and then she stood aside and watched as I went all *Blue Peter* on her.

The idea was simple. Firstly I threaded the bottle through the tubigrip and pulled it up my arm, and then I simply reversed the bottle and tucked it under the tubigrip so that it was resting flush to the top of my forearm, with all the tubing and the bottle being held securely in place by the tubigrip. It was like an arm-mounted cannon, but the important thing was that it was securely in place. All that was visible was the tubigrip, the ends of the PICC line and valve end of the bottle. Plus it was really comfortable (well as comfortable as could be expected) and would allow me to dress, shower and sleep without having to continuously worry about where to put the bottle or whether it was safe or not. Jane looked less than convinced as I stood in the middle of the ward waving my left arm about triumphantly.

"See! Sorted! Look I can even button my cuffs down on my shirt. This is the way forward I'm telling ya. I'll tell you what – you can have this idea on the house, however next time I will have to charge you." I said with a massive cat got the cream and the budgie grin on my face.

"Hmmm," hmmmed Jane.

"Just be careful with it. I want to see you on Monday to check that everything is all right and change your dressings; apart from that you can go," she said.

"Thanks, you are a star. I'm off to the office to show them my new little friend," I said excitedly.

And with that I left the hospital still being able to wear my suit and not have anyone looking strangely at me because I've tubes protruding from everywhere. Life was good. I don't want you to think that I am an overtly vain person it's just that one of the hardest side-effects for me to cope with during my having cancer was the leper syndrome. I had by this stage gotten used to saying that I had cancer and in fact I made an effort not to merely say I was ill but actually say the word cancer. Almost without exception it was a bit of a conversation killer. "Oh! Err! Sorry to hear that. Oh is that the time – got to be going. *Taxi!*" and that would be that. People just don't want to talk about it unless of course they, a friend or family member has suffered or indeed died of cancer.

I found the social implications initially were harder to deal with than the cancer itself. I don't know if this is just me, or a male perspective or what. It seemed to me that certain cancers were more acceptable to talk about. For example, breast cancer has a lot of press, and rightly so. It almost seems that if you are unfortunate enough to have suffered with this devastating disease, the support from pretty much everyone in society is already in place, almost as if you are part of a "sisterhood". Perhaps this is because women are better at discussing their fears and emotions than men. Whatever the reason, I felt as if I had a rather uncool cancer; arse cancer just doesn't have that certain *je ne sais pas!* Rachel thought the new arm mounted bottle was a definite step in the right direction when I showed up at the office. In fact I was so happy with it I went and did a couple of interviews for some of the other managers just to see if the interviewees would notice the bottle under my shirt. Not a dickey bird! I waited for Rachel and we retired home for the night. To celebrate the arrival of my new little friend, and the fact that I still felt absolutely fine all things considered, I decided that we should have a takeaway.

This might seem like a bit of a strange call to make on the eve of receiving a new dose of chemo, but as I have already mentioned I didn't want to let my illness rule my life. I had obviously made some alterations: I had stopped smoking cigarettes (unless I was in the pub, which I had not been to much since my revelation), swapped Stella for red wine, and in considerably less quantity than prior to being ill, and generally had tried to improve my lifestyle. This was all very well and good, but I did not feel any worse than before falling ill, plus I also felt that it was a bit unfair on Rachel. I was the one who had the tumour but there were two of us having to live with the cancer, and whilst I do not think that for a second Rachel cared a toss as to whether we had a takeaway or a healthier option, it was important for my own sanity, as much as anything else, to act as normally as possible for as long as possible.

We plumped for the Indian option and I went for the most innocuous dish I could find. Whilst I felt well, my arse had continued to be vociferous in its reaction to a large tumour growing within its vicinity. Rachel warned me that this was probably a bad idea, but I insisted, and within forty-five minutes we were settled down ready to eat like any normal couple and watch a film. Within sixty-five minutes I was on the bog - I had barely had time to finish the onion bhaji and start my main course, when my stomach grumbled a warning and that was the end of my night.

"Rachel. Could you bring me a glass of water up please?" I shouted through the bathroom door from my throne. My flat was only a small one-bedroom affair, with a spiral staircase connecting the open plan lounge–kitchen to the upstairs, which housed the bedroom and a small bathroom. Rachel popped her head around the door and proffered me the pint of water. "How ya feeling?" she enquired with genuine concern.

"Mental note – when receiving treatment for cancer of the colon DO NOT have an Indian," I said draining the entire pint of water, before swivelling towards the sink, refilling the pint and draining half of that as well.

"I don't understand. You had only just started the meal – how could it go through you so quickly?" offered Rachel.

"No idea, but I don't think that I'm going to be downstairs for a while; might as well start the movie without me. I'll be fine," I said as another wave of intense pain washed through my gut.

"Feels like period pains!" I said with a smile, trying to ease Rachel's concerns.

"Honest, go watch the movie and I'll be down as soon as…!" I suggested. Rachel reluctantly retired to the lounge leaving me to ponder the subtle nuances of chemotherapy. This is when I realised that I was not going to be able to blithely sail through this thing and would have to think about my body a lot more. I have always been aware of how my body reacts and feels, but now I had to learn how to really listen to what it was telling me. And at that moment it was telling me that I was a dickhead and that takeaways were a no-go. I have to admit to agreeing with my body 100% at that point.

CHAPTER 16: RADIO GA-GA

The rest of the weekend was a bit of a write-off. I spent most of it on the bog. By Sunday evening my stomach was fine, and by the time I went to the hospital on the Monday morning (the 8th of September), my arse had quietened down as well, relatively speaking. My first stop was to pop in and see Jane to have my dressings changed and check that the infuser was working properly. With that all done and dusted I was off to get nuked for the first time at the radiotherapy department, which was located in another part of the hospital.

The radiotherapy department's waiting area, owing to the nature of the treatment, was situated on the ground floor of the outbuilding, away from the treatment areas themselves that were down in the basement. After checking in at the reception window, I made my way through the glass doors of the waiting room and made myself comfy. Once again I was by far the youngest person in the room, and once again I felt guilty that I wasn't as ill as most of my fellow patients. Cancer, all of my joviality aside, can be a devastating illness, and unfortunately as is often the way in life, fire is met with fire, and therefore the treatments can be just as devastating. Like chemotherapy, radiotherapy has its fair share of side-effects all of which will depend on your general health, type of treatment and the positioning of the area to be irradiated. As I have already mentioned, I was to receive external radiation treatment, which was of course centred on my lower regions. The core side -effects are primarily the same:

- Sickness,
- Loss of appetite, and
- Skin irritation of the affected areas.

Obviously, with my tumour being where it was, i.e. up me bum, it was likely that I would suffer with diarrhoea, discomfort around the old chocolate starfish, and the possibility that I might experience some pain when going for a wee! The idea was that the combined potency of the continuous 24/7 chemo and thirty consecutive sessions of radiotherapy would have the desired effect upon the tumour, allowing doctors Myint and Hershman to work their magic. Fingers crossed!

Hospitals are essentially run on procedures, so my first contact with the nursing staff was to go through my personal details again. For some reason, it doesn't matter how often you give your details – they are almost always wrong. This is not only irritating but must cost a fortune – a national database would be an idea, so they would at least all have the same wrong information! Then I was introduced to the staff nurse who would be having "little chats" with me every couple of days all the way through my treatment, to make sure that all was well. Then back to the waiting room to wait, and wait and just for good measure a dash of waiting. I had just begun to wonder if all these old people in the waiting room had arrived that old, when I was called.

I was instructed to take the lift to the basement, turn left once out of the lift and head for the radiotherapy machine called VIV. (There were several machines all with little names: TEX, VIC and LEVI.) When I stepped out of the lift it was like entering a nuclear bunker with glass fronted offices and the telltale paint job – murky yellowy/greyish sort of colour. I headed left to the end of the corridor where there was a small seating area and a control desk that had more monitors, lights and buttons than the bridge of the Enterprise. There were three nurses having a chat and sharing a tin of chocs.

"Ooo! Sweeties. Any of those purple ones left – you know the one with the nut in?" I enquired. Six slightly surprised eyes instantly levelled themselves at me.

"That'll be a no then!"

"And you are?" asked one of the nurses, obviously the boss, in a South African accent. I introduced myself and gave them my newly updated records. "I'm here to be nuked," I informed her. The two young Asian nurses sniggered, and I thought I saw an attempt at a smirk on the face of the "Boss". I was offered and accepted a seat, and took in my surroundings. The room was circular, like a glass bubble at the end of a blowing pipe, with TV monitors arranged on the far wall that would allow the staff to observe the treatment from afar. Just in front of where I was sitting, and taking up most of the room's floor space, was the aforementioned control desk, all curved with monitors and dials, and a tin of Quality Street.

One of the nurses, Raj, appeared in the corridor and called me to follow her into the treatment room. Off the main corridor to the right was a pair of large grey doors that you would in normal circumstances avoid owing to the impressive array of danger and radiation signs affixed to it. I was left in no doubt that this was the entrance to the radiotherapy room. I was led down a curving corridor that opened up into the main treatment room itself. The room was pretty large, with a battery of medical looking things along the opposite wall to the entrance. In the centre of the room was a table that could be moved to the exact position and height required by my positioning tattoos in order to affect the most damage to the tumour. The radiation device itself looked like a cross between one of those robots in a car factory and something from *Terminator*. It was about seven to eight feet high with a pyramidal base, and an arm that stretched out over the table. The arm held the gun bit – not its proper name but it was the bit that was about to shoot me. I was asked to remove my shoes and trousers, and once again hop onto the bed – not on my left side, knees up you'll be glad to hear; just plain old lying on my front.

Before we could proceed with the nuking I had to be positioned to the nearest millimetre. This was achieved by lining my tattoos up with a laser that emanated from two of the sidewalls. My boxers were rolled halfway down my bum to expose the tattoos and the positioning began.

"Seeing as this is your first visit, this will take a little longer than normal. Once done we will be able to set the table up a lot quicker for your next treatment," explained the Boss! "So please stay as still as you can."

"OK!" was all I could manage, as I was really quite comfy and felt like having a little snooze. Although the table could move up and down it wasn't very good at alternative directions so I was rudely awakened from my attempted snooze by cold hands shifting my arse unceremoniously about.

"Aah! Haaannndddsss!" I eeked.

"Stop moaning!" said Boss.

"I'm not moaning," I moaned. "It was just a bit of a shock that's all." The Boss went to set some other stuff up while Raj and her colleague took over. Their hands were a lot warmer and I settled back to allow these two lovely young ladies to stroke and move me gently into position. I have to admit that having to turn up for a month of this didn't seem as bad as I had first suspected – no impaling with digits, lightsabers or any other implement whatsoever. In fact there was no lube to be seen. Believe me that whilst you might be sitting there thinking "Old perv", I can assure you that, although admittedly being positioned by a couple of attractive young nurses was quite nice, this was the only time apart from the fertility clinic where I could relax and enjoy myself without the threat of being buggered. Small mercies maybe, but with cancer you take what you can get.

"All done," announced Boss. "We will leave the room and watch from the waiting area. The treatment will last around ten minutes and then we will come and get you. Any questions?"

"No," I mumphed. My cheek was flush to the plastic covering of the table and lifting my head to answer was a no-no. Even the smallest movement could affect my overall positioning, and this would result in the reintroduction of the cold hands every time I moved my head a little. So, as the staff fled to the safety of their nuclear bunker, I just lay there, pants halfway down my bum with a little pool of drool forming by the corner of my cheek flush to the table.

The robotic arm spent the next ten minutes orbiting my partially exposed moon, accompanied by an intermittent high pitched shrill when the machine was doing its thing. The robotic arm ceased its orbit, coming to rest directly above my bum. Silence! The girls came back in and moved the treatment table from under the radiotherapy machine and then informed me that it was all finished and that I could pull my pants back up. "We'll see you in the reception when you're all done!" said Boss. Thankful, I sat up, quickly wiping away the little pool of drool, and dressed myself. Back in the control room we organised the roster for my treatment over the next five weeks. I plumped for the four in the afternoon slot as this would allow me to pop into the office in the morning whilst I was still able, and give me time enough to get to the hospital when I wasn't. Thanking the girls, I left for the day thinking that all in all this radiotherapy stuff was a bit of a doddle. Oh how wrong I was, but as I might have mentioned earlier, sometimes ignorance is bliss.

CHAPTER 17: THESE BOOTS WERE MADE FOR WALKING!

It was the morning of Tuesday the 9th of September. Rachel had gone to work, and I had tried in vain, owing to the extremely noisy road outside my window, to have a bit of a lie- in. I lay on my back in bed, positioned in traditional manner of someone who's partner has got up and gone to work – the starfish – and prepared myself for the day ahead. "No major dramas today," I thought. "I'll pop into the office and then off for a bit of a nuking," absent-mindedly itching under the tubigrip which held my chemo filled arm mounted cannon. I looked at my arm and smiled – funny what you can get used to!

It had only been seven weeks since I had been told that I had cancer, and in that time I'd been prodded, impaled, digitally abused and nearly eviscerated. I'd travelled around the country trying to find alternatives to the "bum deal" I'd been offered, and found a potential treatment that wasn't really designed for people my age and might not work anyway. "And, why am I so damn hot?"

The extraordinary summer of 2003 was rolling over into a glorious Indian summer, which would have been great if I wasn't connected 24/7 to a chemo dispenser. For some reason, since the two weekend sessions with the 5FU, I had been suffering more than usual with the heat. And although I'd only had this extremely toxic chemical flowing through my veins continuously for a few days, things were definitely afoot – and I don't mean in the Kingdom of Denmark. It was as if my body had thrown out its internal thermometer, and proclaimed *Let There Be Sweat* and lo, there was sweat.

"Sod it!" I said getting out of bed – there would be no rest for me today. I looked back at the bed sheets and could see what looked like a sweaty imprint of Da Vinci's Vitruvian Man. "That's just not right!" I said to myself, whilst shaking my head. I donned my plastic arm protector and showered, before attempting to clean my teeth with the front twelve bristles of the brush. The ulcers and the various new lergies that had come to party on my under siege lips had meant that, apart from looking like Bubba from Forrest Gump, it had gotten very difficult to talk, eat or even clean my teeth properly. However, as I pottered downstairs, I considered myself a pretty lucky chap. I had a cancer that was diagnosed early and treatable; the only downsides so far being temperature control problems, moody mouth sores. Oh! And, a hole in my left arm, with a pipe leading from above my heart, to a bottle containing a cell destroying liquid, which was attached to my arm. Apart from that I was peachy!

Breakfast: the most important meal of the day. To be honest I had not taken breakfast seriously (this does not, of course, include mandatory post-Saturday night fry-up down the local café or at home if the appropriate girlfriend bribes were in place) since I was a child. However, since my diet was the most likely cause of the cancer residing up me bum, I had made a conscious effort to establish some resemblance of a routine. This started with Shreddies eaten with great care owing to their sharp corners – sore lips remember. Obviously, since the near pants-based catastrophe that occurred the last time I'd attempted pure orange juice, it was tea all the way for this boy, I can tell ya! Then it was off to the office, followed by a leisurely bum stroke and nuking session down at St. Barts. This lasted for exactly a week and then things started to go "Pete Tong" in a hurry.

Towards the end of the first full week of treatment I noticed that my body had started to react to the onslaught of the drugs coursing through my system. The slight tingle in my hands had escalated to full blown Ow! The sensation reminded me of being at school – that slapped hand feeling that you get when you are in goal, in the winter, without gloves and some smart arse blasts the football at you from five yards away. Only multiplied by ten. Whilst this did hurt quite a lot and made holding things – especially cups of hot drink – quite difficult, it wasn't incapacitating.

Have you ever been to a child's party or a holiday camp with a less than great magician proclaiming with great gusto, "And now for my next trick?" This was the start of my second week of full-time treatment to a T. As my hands started to return to normal size and sensitivity, my feet thought that it was time for them to get involved. In the past I had worked in various service industries and even door-to-door sales, so the odd blister on my feet was something I had plenty of experience of. Nothing like this though; this was different. The soles of my feet started to get extremely sensitive to any pressure whatsoever. It was not so much a tingle, but a burning sensation at first with which I was fine. The next stage, just in time for my mum's visit to London for my birthday, was the appearance of blood blisters on the balls of my feet. We've all had the odd blood blister, and, whilst uncomfortable, they are not crippling and so I wasn't unduly concerned.

By the seventeenth, my birthday, the entire surface of the balls of my feet and toes were covered in a giant blood blister. The reasons for this form of Palmer planters are not exactly known, although it is slightly more common when the chemotherapy is administered via an infusion pump. I have a completely non-professional theory which runs along the lines that if chemo prevents new cells being made, it makes sense that with every step taken you might kill cells in your feet, especially the parts of your feet that you land and take off with i.e. balls and heels. If these cells don't get replaced, they form blood blisters and, *et voilà*, 60% of your feet are covered in a massive, extremely sensitive, and enlarged blister. Walking was a joke! I have no idea whether this theory is correct but the fact remained that the parts of my feet that were used for walking were not happy bunnies.

Mum arrived at Euston Train Station, and we decided that it might be nice to pop down to the Thames and have a bite to eat. She rang me from Euston and we agreed that an area called Embankment in London would be the ideal meeting place, close to the river and accessible by tube. Before leaving the house, I had to undergo a fairly extensive checklist of considerations in preparation for the journey. Firstly, the location of tubes and local establishments where I could have emergency poo breaks. Sounds daft, but I cannot stress enough that, as the treatment increased, the delay time between "Oo! I need a poo!" and "Oo! I need new pants!" decreased dramatically. There was the obvious "What to wear" issue. It was my mum after all and having cancer was no excuse for being scruffy. And, in view of my current foot situation, footwear was crucial. Now, I have a male footwear theory, and it is just purely a theory, but here it is anyway. There are two types of bloke: you have your shoes and boots wearer; and you have your trainer wearer. Whilst it is obvious that from time to time both camps will wear the other's footwear, the acid test is an evening out with the girlfriend or maybe the lads. You will either pop some shoes, or, in my case more likely, boots, on, because subconsciously you will have a minimum level of acceptable appearance, or you will stick your white Reeboks on with your blue jeans and Ben Sherman shirt and walk around like you've just got off a very large horse. However, when your feet are covered with an inordinately painful blood blister, the odd fashion faux pas is the least of your worries.

Whilst I had over the previous couple of days attempted to wear my trainers because of the increased comfort and internal padding, I had found that my feet had tended to move around in the trainers, and therefore aggravate the blisters even more. This meant that even a simple potter around down by the Thames might need another approach, and it was gonna hurt. I opted for my boots. Apart from the fact that they went well with what I was wearing, there was some logic to the move. I was often told that a good way to still the pain from a blood blister or a bruise was to apply pressure to the hurt area. With the boots, although they have solid soles, the elevation of the heel and the contour of the toe-end meant that the balls of my feet would be held relatively still. This did however hurt like "mother fuck", but at least the pain was constant, and that meant that I could try to shut it out to some extent. So I gingerly set off to meet Mum down by the river, via the odd public convenience.

Once outside Embankment Tube Station I called Mum to find where she had wandered off to, and then made my way to the café where she was. In order to get to her I had to negotiate a fairly steep slope down to the river. The intensity of the pain grew in conjunction with the steepness of the slope. I saw her standing halfway down the slope looking concerned about my general demeanour. As I approached I shouted that I might not be able to stop. "Are your feet that bad?" she enquired, as I got closer.

"I'm alright once I get a bit of a lick on," I answered as I staggered past her, "but stopping is a bugger," I continued, smiling through the pain.

"See you at the bottom!" I waved, as I careered past like Frank Spencer on roller-skates, without the skates.

"On my way – ah bless!" I heard her call after me.

I eventually reached the road at the bottom, went straight over it without stopping, and came to rest against the railing at the river's edge. Mum caught up, gave me a big birthday hug, and made lots of Ooo-ing and Aah-ing noises about my condition, and generally made me feel a lot better. Once I had reassured her that I was perfectly fine, give or take the odd sore foot, which was nothing for her to worry about whatsoever, we started to look for a place to eat. There are several really nice restaurant barges that are permanently docked along the side of the Thames, so we hopped onto the first one with some spare tables on deck and ordered.

It was a glorious, shirtsleeves rolled up sort of day. My radiotherapy had been cancelled, owing to the machine 'VIV' having a bit of a turn, whatever that meant. I felt that I could allow myself the odd glass of wine, so we plumped for a nice Pinot Grigio. After about half an hour the heat was starting to get to me. Although not completely full, the boat had no tables free with shade left; this meant that I was sitting in direct sunlight with a bottle of rapidly warming toxic liquid being fed into my system. This, as you can imagine, wasn't good. "It feels like the heat is boiling my chemo," I ventured in a light-hearted way. The last thing that I would want would be to make Mum any more anxious about my situation than she already was, so I simply suggested that the next spare table that came available should be made ours. Once in the shade we set about the wine and talked like we hadn't for a long time.

We agreed that whatever we were going to do that day it would be within staggering distance for my sake. I don't think that I had walked that much in ages by the end of the day. Firstly, we crossed the Thames over to the Satchi museum with its weird cut up cows. Then off to the Dali exhibition, which was excellent, if not considerably strange, and then back over the river to the side we started on. We walked up towards Covent

Garden, via a chemist to buy some foam pads for the balls of my feet, which by this time had gone so far past painful that it no longer mattered how far we walked – like the point you reach when walking in torrential rain without a brolly, only drier. The circuit that we took was probably only a couple of square kilometres but it hurt like buggery. However, the more I found the pain increasing the more of a joke I tried to make it, not only for my mum or indeed Rachel's sake, but for myself. No one dies from a sore foot, well not very often, and in comparison to some of the other patients that I had seen, I still felt extremely lucky, if not a tad tender.

It was a great day! In a way it's sad that people sometimes only appreciate the simple things like spending time with loved ones, going for a walk or a bite to eat, when confronted with potential disaster. Mum made her way back up north to Chester while I hobbled back to my little flat and a bowl of water to pop my feet in.

The rest of the week was a bit of a struggle, not because I had gotten worse dramatically or anything; I was just struggling with the things that you take for granted – walking, eating, going to the toilet, etc. So I went to work on the Friday for the last time during my treatment. Although I had closed the business and had nothing to really do at the office, I felt that psychologically it was important to make the effort to be active. Without sounding like a bit of a girl, I had to admit that the amount of pain that my feet were causing me meant that the extra walking involved with just getting to the office, let alone the four stories of steps within the building itself, made it almost physically prohibitive. Plus, they never had any bog roll, which for a man in my condition is an important factor to take into account. So I bid my farewells and settled into pottering about the house and doing nothing – bar going to Barts to get nuked every day and playing on the Xbox obviously.

CHAPTER 18: PARK LIFE

The thing about cancer that I found most strange was that, like most people, I was aware of the standard treatments i.e. chemo and radiotherapy, and the standard effects of this treatment: hair loss, weight loss, fatigue and so on. I was prepared for these to happen, although I was extremely happy that my hair was still in place, and the fact that I had extra room in my trousers wasn't a total negative; a lot easier "so far" than going to the gym to lose weight. Even the severe blistering of my feet, ulceration of my lips and mouth, and the sensitivity of my hands were, if not pleasant, not totally surprising. It's the little things that I found most interesting! As the summer had gotten hotter and hotter, I had started to drink water like it was going out of fashion. Nothing interesting there, you might say, and you'd be right. However, since I'd started with the continuous treatment, I found that I couldn't drink certain brands of bottled water. Whilst I won't name names, I can confirm the company's claims that the water within each bottle has come from the depths of a volcano because I could bloody taste it.

Also, like thousands of people in this country, I suffer, only on my scalp luckily, with psoriasis. For those who don't know psoriasis it's like eczema with attitude, and, because I have it under my hair, when the skin gets irritated it flakes off. It's like mega dandruff – not so much Head and Shoulders as Head on Shoulders. With the chemo, supposedly, killing pretty much every replicating cell in my body, the psoriasis went completely. Whilst I'm definitely not advocating chemo as a way to battle psoriasis, (primarily because it does come back with a vengeance once the treatment has finished, which would be a serious case of overkill if you ask me), it was nevertheless quite interesting, not to mention a brief respite for my head.

Monday 22nd September was the start of my third week of treatment. After hobbling in to see Jane to get my arm hairs ripped out again, and a new bottle fixed into place, I was off to my nuking. At the beginning and end of each week I had an appointment either with the staff nurse or with the assistant to the ever-elusive radiologist to discuss my progress. This particular afternoon it was the turn of the doctor to assess me. To my surprise the doctors and, to some degree, the nursing staff, weren't too concerned about lips, hands or feet, although I didn't really mention the feet thing too much – stiff upper lip and all that, old chap! What they were questioning me on was my lower regions, and whether I had much discomfort when going to the loo or irritation of the skin. I had to admit that the majority of the "strangeness" that I had experienced so far was predominately chemo-based. This didn't stop the doctor going through the "Poo Chart" with me again. The Poo Chart is a list of ten different types of poos that you could have, pictorially represented in amazing Technicolor on a handy A4 laminated (for easy cleaning) piece of paper. I'd partaken in at least 60% of the list so far. I'd had most of the usual suspects – the logs, submarines, floaters, nut clusters, the noisy but somehow strangely satisfying botty-orgasm or exploding arse; and now had even progressed on to the multi-Malteaser bowel filler. Obviously these are not the medical terms for them, although I think they should be. No real problems though mentally I had been preoccupied with the fact that I couldn't walk. I was given some Paracetamol for my feet – cheers then – and for any future skin discomfort, and sent on my way to get nuked. After nuking, I was given some cream to put on my skin around my thighs and lower regions in general; and some stuff called Intra-cite gel that was dispensed from yet another mushroom shaped receptacle. No up, this time, just on and around thankfully, and best served chilled straight from the fridge. With that pearl of wisdom I retired home, only to return the next day and do it all over again.

Whilst repetition is, by its very nature, boring, I found that my days were beginning to take some recognisable form, and this was in its own way quite comforting. It meant that I could concentrate on the parts of my body, and not my day, that were giving me grief. I cannot emphasise enough the role that the nurses and radiotherapy staff had on my new-found inner calm. Jane and Chris at my chemo ward, and Raj and the rest of the girls who nuked me every day have to deal with unbelievable levels of stress and emotion every day, but somehow make sure that you are the most important person when they deal with the individual. They do more than help cure people; they help people heal both mentally and physically.

However, since finishing work, properly this time, I had managed to finish my *Star Wars* game (chemo has no detrimental affects on your ability to wield a lightsaber and use the force) and did find myself with a lot of dead time. Luckily, the weather was still holding and this allowed me to get out of my little flat and potter gingerly down to the local park, read and get some badly needed vitamin D from the sunlight. On a couple of occasions the local infant school had playtime at a kiddies area within the park. I don't have kids, and to be honest hadn't really considered them at this point of my life. I always wanted to make sure that I could afford to have them before going forth and multiplying (foolish I know!)

Watching small children play, though, is the best thing in the world; they truly are "little people" without the neuroses. Sitting there in a park, at the age of only thirty-two, with a bottle of chemotherapy strapped to my arm, waiting for the time to pass before having to have radiation shot at me, was an immensely sobering and emotional moment. Once again it was the "What the hell am I doing here?" sort of thoughts running through my mind. What have I achieved as an individual? What impact has my life had, if any, on others? Have I been a positive or negative example of a human being? Had I strayed to the "Dark Side"? Not believing in heaven and hell, this wasn't a religious mental conversation; it was more of a personal checklist of my life's progress since having a clean slate like the kids I was watching.

The kids just didn't have a care in the world, bar whose turn it was on the swing, or whether to play with Jordan or Mohammed. I couldn't help myself smiling at their antics and their sheer willingness to engage in play with anything and anyone. What I found most inspiring is the fact that children are colour blind. They don't care if the other kid is a different colour or religion because they haven't been taught prejudice yet. Life seems a lot simpler for them; if they don't like someone it's for no other reason than they don't like them. This state of friendship or not could, and probably does, change daily, if not hourly, but nevertheless it seems, if not fairer, a lot less cynical. They were funny, and they gave me hope that ignorance isn't genetic; it's learned, and our planet might yet survive. Do you want to know what the most upsetting thing was, from my point of view? I only went to that part of the park twice, because I felt that people might have thought that I was some sort of perv, because I was sitting within visual distance of the kids, and – dare I say it – smiling. Guilt seems to affect the innocent a lot more than the guilty in today's society, with those who perpetrate crimes seemingly protected more than the victims. I tended to get emotional during my treatment, and with the reality that death was a possibility came a great clarity of thought. I kept thinking of the story of the British and German soldiers playing football during the

Great War, before resuming hostilities; "Too little too late" will be written as the earth's final epitaph.

So, with a renewed sense of live-and-let-live, I went and bought a new game for the Xbox, *Halo*, and showed the advancing hoards of aliens exactly what I thought of intergalactic relations. By the end of the third week of treatment my hands had completely cleared up, and the blood blisters on my feet had started to dry out and not hurt as much. Things were looking up.

CHAPTER 19: AND NOW FOR SOMETHING COMPLETELY DIFFERENT!

The start of the fourth week however, brought some new and unexpected developments. Firstly, one of the favourite conversations of the staff nurse, when having our little one-to-ones, was my sex life, or lack thereof. I thought that I was doing my bit, all things considered, but it was a valid line of questioning. As I mentioned earlier, living with the cancer was for me not too hard because of the tremendous support around me. And the sex question was more about how my illness was affecting Rachel's life, as opposed to whether I was still feeling horny whilst my feet, lips, gums and hands blistered. So, I decided to make a conscious effort that night and "get jiggy with it".

Without going into, shall we say, blow-by-blow detail, I noticed that my "old boy" looked bigger than usual. Excellent, I thought – chemo gives you a bigger dick. I was, however, wrong! What chemo *does* do is make your hair fall out – mine just didn't fall off my head, that's all. I hadn't noticed because – this might sound strange but "bare" with me – I'd spent the majority of the last few weeks looking backwards when going to the loo. The Poo List was to be completed if at all possible – little personal goal not essential for recovery from colon cancer. I hadn't been concentrating on the rest of my plumbing, and at some time over the past fortnight or so all of my pubic hair had fallen off. I was completely bald. No *back, sack and crack* wax needed by me. It was like a bag of giblets without the bag – sexy!

Now, men's propensity for preferring a lady's genital hair to be named after South American natives is well known – nothing worse than impromptu flossing I always say. Luckily for me it seemed that the feeling was a mutual one, or so Rachel assured me.

"Oh! Baby, all of your pubes have gone," laughed Rachel. "Looks bigger though," she added enthusiastically, smiling. "Do you think it still works?" she enquired with added impishness.

"Suppose we'd better find out," I replied, grinning insanely. Game On! So feeling smoother and more streamlined, I proceeded to see if everything still worked, and thankfully it did. Remember, where there's a willy, there's a way!

Have you ever heard the old adage that "the best way to get rid of a headache is to be kicked in the shin?" The idea is that the pain of the leg will refocus your attention, and you'll forget about the headache. Well, that was the chemo/radio duo's next trick; my skin around my entire lower regions began to heat up thanks to the daily treatment – radiation burns as well as killing cancer cells. My skin had started to heat up quite dramatically over the course of that fourth week. Up until that point there hadn't been the slightest indication of what was about to happen to my poor arse – not a dickybird! Suddenly going the toilet was beginning to hurt more than usual. I had the cream and started to apply it twice a day to the tattooed areas around my thighs, but the burning sensation when on the bog meant that I was in need of more than cream and Paracetamol.

It was now the 1st of October and the effects that had started to manifest themselves as a result of the treatment had started to exert more control on my everyday life. At my midweek meeting with the doctor I brought up the subject of my rapidly deteriorating arse. He examined my poor posterior and upgraded my medication, improved painkillers and some steroid-based suppositories, which I wasn't over the moon about. Talk about going straight to the point of pain. By the Friday it had gotten worse – a lot worse. The skin around and up my bum crack, along with that sensitive area under me goolies had started to turn black from the radiation burns. Aside from that, my insides felt as if they weren't faring much better than my outsides.

The doctor gave me some local anaesthetic cream called Lignocaine (essentially Bongella for your arse), and the nurses gave me loads of Intra-cite gel-filled parcels which looked again like "mushrooms", and some reusable gel packs, both to be applied directly to my undercarriage. The little gel packs looked like clear processed cheese slices; same size and thickness – just that you put them on your arse instead of your burgers. The inside of my fridge was becoming a very crowded place. I had pure Aloe Vera gel – excellent on the burns when cold – the gel packs and mushrooms all chilling ready to be applied to my now blackened, and beginning to crack and fall off, skin. As you might have noticed, I'm a big believer in every cloud having a silver lining, and admittedly finding one in the "my skin is being systematically burnt to a crisp" cloud was tricky, but one was found nonetheless. The best thing about all of these gels and creams was that they had to be applied, and to be honest the areas affected weren't in the easiest places to reach. So, if you had wandered into my lounge of an evening during that final week or so, you might well have wondered what sort of den of iniquity had you wandered in to. There was I, laid back on the couch, sarong up around my waist, legs akimbo, *sans* underwear with Rachel knelt on the floor between my thighs, head appearing and disappearing from view. Rachel's family have a fantastic saying for when you know you are in a serious relationship and you are comfortable with one another completely – you are "Farting Familiar".

"Oh baby, your skin is totally burnt black, and it's beginning to split," Rachel informed me sounding genuinely concerned for my well-being.

"Oo! That's cold," I squealed.

"Where else?" enquired Rachel from between my thighs.

"Everywhere … down a bit, left … ahhhhhh! There's ya boy!" It was really quite nice, better even than cold aftersun on holiday shoulders.

"Do you want some bum Bongella on as well?" Rachel's head appeared in my reclined line of vision again. I opted for the Aloe Vera gel option, wanting to save the Lignocaine for when things got really bad. I'd take as much pain as was possible and only use the "good stuff" for breakthrough pain – sort of similar in thinking to not wearing your coat indoors because when you go outside you won't feel the advantage.

"You know your mum's saying about being 'farting familiar'?" I gasped as a new layer of cold gel was applied.

"Yes," said Rachel concentrating on the "job at hand".

"Well we've sooo passed that point, in a big way. We've moved straight onto smearing chilled gel on my bollocks stage – how cool's that?" I couldn't believe what had happened to me over the past few months, and the fact that Rachel was there, strong, and going well beyond the call of duty at that moment was astonishing to me.

As I lay there on the couch, having gel applied to my sore bum and balls, I once again felt very, very lucky that I wasn't in this alone, and I had people who loved me and would be there for me.

Once basted, we settled down for the evening. Rachel grabbed the beanbag and I lay back on the couch, the sarong forming a little tent over my nicely chilling thighs allowing the cool autumn breeze blowing through the window to cool my bits even further – silver lining: not 'alf.

By the start of the fifth and final week things had progressed from a pain in the arse to serious hurt. I was now experiencing extreme pain every time I went for a number two even though I had put myself on a low residue diet to minimise the amount of solid wastage being passed. The hospital had given me no dietary advice during my treatment, just drugs. Whilst I was grateful for the drugs, I had major concerns about the amount of different pills that I'd been given to take; I'd restricted myself, so far, to using the painkillers only for extreme pain control. The registrar, however, wasn't thinking outside of the box, concentrating only on dealing with the symptoms and not looking for other areas that could have been improved. I mentioned the dramatic increase in discomfort when on the loo at our Monday meeting, and in all fairness to the registrar, we discussed options as to whether a laxative or something to back me up a bit might help the situation; I was going to the loo at least eight to ten times a day and it had gotten past a joke. I didn't like the idea of going to the loo more because, to be honest, I could have pooed a peanut and it would have felt like I was giving birth to an elephant out of my arse and the idea of saving it all up for a "mega jobbie" was just not worth even contemplating. So we plumped for Plan C, Morphine – accept no imitation! I eventually received several bottles of a liquid morphine from the hospital's pharmacy. The hospital pharmacy could make a sloth look like it had a sense of urgency – really quite impressively slow – it must take some training and discipline to be that slow; in fact it would make an interesting nature/nurture case study – is being crap learned or genetic? Four hours, I kid you not!

By midweek I could feel my shield of invincibility slipping; I was beginning to crack under the constant pain. The burning from my skin was nothing compared with the pain of actually going to the loo. And just to keep me on my toes, I'd now started to pee blood – nice. I virtually stopped eating. I was literally scared to go to the loo, but I knew that this was the price to be paid for saving my arse, and so I had to find a way to deal with it. As I mentioned I was not entirely happy with the idea of idly throwing more drugs at the problems that were caused by too many drugs in my system in the first place – if that makes any sense at all? I had sleeping tablets, tranquillisers, hardcore painkillers and morphine, all of which I would need to have taken continually if I was going to be able to cope with the searing pain. Of course this would mean that having a conversation with me would be like talking to the microwave; I'd just sit there making a steady humming noise, with the occasional "ping" for good measure!

So I decided to go old school and smoke cannabis. I don't want to get into a socio-political debate over the pros and cons of the legalisation of the drug, but it helped me. I found that my anxiety level dropped, and so did the never-ending discomfort. The pain was still there but it lacked the edge that had previously made it almost incapacitating. This meant that it was manageable and that is all you can ask for really. I didn't want Rachel and my mum to see the real physical cost of the treatment. They had enough to deal with, especially Rachel who had extra bum gelling duties to contend with. The flip side of this stoned coin is that it meant not eating very much was much more difficult – munchies!

I did obviously still take the odd painkiller or swig of morphine when it got too much to handle, and more often than not the worst of the pain came post-nuking. I don't know if my insides are psychic or something, but almost always prior to actually being nuked my insides would want out. I remember on several occasions experiencing the infamous "repeating poo", which is where you go, finish, wipe and stand,

and even leave the loo, when "aftershock", and you're back on the loo again; not once, but three or four times in a row. And after the radiotherapy session, anything left in my colon would not be best pleased, and would be hell-bent on inflicting as much agony as a poo could inflict upon my oh-so-stinging ring.

"Raaa-ch. Could you bring me a cold pint of water up?" I called from my flat's toilet.

"Do you want ice?"

"No thanks, just run the tap a while. Cheers honey!" I called from my throne.

I had only a couple of days left of the radiotherapy according to the original diary I was given, but this schedule had been altered earlier that day. During the previous five weeks the radiotherapy machine had broken on a couple of occasions, which meant that I was playing catch-up until the middle of the next week. This had a knock-on effect on the rest of my medical diary. I was due to visit Liverpool the following Tuesday to see Dr Myint about proceeding with the Papillon radiotherapy, and this had to be cancelled. I have to admit that this wasn't a problem in my book by any means. I had planned to cancel the appointment anyway, owing to the sorry state that my arse was in and being only too aware of the propensity for inserting objects up patients' arses that oncologists seem to share. There was not even the remotest chance of me allowing anything to be put anywhere near my ring of fire. I had tried the suppositories once, a couple of days previously, and my arse spat them out like a child being force-fed Brussels sprouts; my bum was strictly one-way traffic for the foreseeable future.

"Thanks honey," I said gratefully retrieving the pint of cold water from her. I leant forward and poured the entire pint down my butt crack. I'm convinced that I could hear the hiss of steam as the water washed over the burnt landscape of my arse.

"Arrrh! Bisto! Oh man that's better."

"Top-up?"

"Love one, thanks." It was like shitting molten lava (or if you're an evil genius living in a hollow volcano – "Magma"). It felt as if the very food that was left in my bowel during the radiotherapy had been nuked, or micro-waved if you prefer, and was literally being delivered piping hot – not good!

Friday the 11th: the last official day of treatment. I made my way to see Jane at Padgett Ward to have an extra half a week's chemo attached to my arm in order to cover the extra few days of the radiotherapy that I'd missed. The idea being that I might as well receive as much treatment as possible; the two worked more effectively when combined. I had no issues with extra chemo, primarily because I knew that the side-effects from the treatment would continue to get worse for the next couple of weeks after the treatment had actually ended, and would in all likelihood last at least another month. I thanked Jane and made my way over to the radiotherapy department. It was near the end of the day and the ward was only half full, which was handy because I was dealt a totally uncalled for "repeating poo" blow.

I only just made it to the toilet and so had no mental preparation time before the onslaught began. I very nearly cried out on several occasions, and probably would have had I not taken a bottle of water with me that was promptly poured down my bum. I had to return to the toilet three more times, refilling and emptying the bottle each time, before I was confident enough to go downstairs to be nuked. The staff could see my discomfort but could do nothing to help me in my plight; this was and always would be my cross to bear and that was that. I thanked them and made my way out of the ward; I was the last to leave and the doors were locked behind me.

Standing outside of the radiotherapy ward, alone and in some degree of discomfort, I tried to listen to what my body was telling me. I had to be completely sure that I would make it either home, or, at the very least, to a designated poo stop along the way before I would attempt the journey home. I dearly hoped I would be OK as I started across the courtyard that led to the other half of the hospital grounds and the way to the tube. I managed 100 yards before a wave of pain swept through my stomach that literally sent me to one knee. Righting myself I tried to think of the closest "clean" public loo. I recalled seeing one just outside of the public canteens within the hospital itself; it was the closest and being in the hospital seemed a safe bet.

I crashed through the doors only to find that out of the two cubicles one was out of order and the other was engaged. My mind raced. I had to be sat down with my trousers around my ankles soon or there would be tears! I leant back against the toilet wall, closed my eyes and attempted to still my mind as well as my breathing – anything to hang on long enough to reach the loo. The cubicle door opened and my eyes snapped back open, my mind now focussed purely on getting past the emerging gentleman. I must have scared the life out of the poor chap who emerged as I dived past him. I slammed the door closed, turning whilst dropping pants, all culminating in an audible roar not only from me but my arse as I made touchdown. Another wave, followed by another and then another; wave after wave of pain flooded my body as my chest sagged onto my knees. My back arched upwards as I forced my head from my knees into the air gasping like someone drowning, not in water but pain.

I cannot really explain the pain that was being generated from simply going to the loo. I was very nearly in tears and was as close to despair as I had been since the commencement of the treatment. Sat there all alone in a little cubicle in Barts Hospital I knew that the searing pain shooting through my entire lower regions, stomach, large and small bowels was doing me good in the long run; but I have to admit that I had serious doubts about the end justifying the means for the first time since I'd found out about the cancer. That was not the only source of internal turmoil raging around my person at that time; there was the age-old battle, not between good and evil as such, but whether I was just being weak or not. I was literally having the little devil vs. little angel on your shoulder type mental conversation with myself; with the devil wanting to go into hospital for the weekend and the angel suggesting that I wasn't that bad and that there were people far more in need of those beds than me.

"I could have myself admitted for the weekend," I thought to myself. *"There would be no shame in that. Lots of people spend time in hospital when receiving cancer treatment!"*

"Pussy!" Not the most backward of angels I admit.

"That's a bit harsh – my arse really hurts! Forty-eight hours of morphine on drip sounds just the ticket."

"Those people in hospital are really old, really ill or most likely – both! You are neither; you're supposed to be laughing at this cancer thing and here you are first sign of trouble and it's off to hospital. Pussy!"

"Doh!" The little devil in me could feel the argument slipping away.

"Exactly. You will just be taking the bed of someone that is really ill. This is what you asked for and this is what you have got. When you're reading the papers on the bog in a year's time this will be history but you will still have an arse."

And that was that! All neuroses apart, I decided to stop being a big girl's blouse and get on with trying to have a dump like a man. After forty-plus minutes of larva logs I made a break for home, to eat some toast and sit in a two-inch deep cold bath with the biggest joint that I could roll – Camberwell Carrot here I come!

CHAPTER 20: MIND SET AND MATCH

"You know your arse is sore when you have a dump and splash-back is a blessing!" I joked to Jonk. We were watching the match at our flat, the day after the moment of weakness, crisis of faith or dabble with the Dark Side – whatever you want to call it. Jonk and Jenny (his girlfriend) had popped round on that Saturday afternoon to see how we were both doing, and I had decided to get back on with beating the cancer the only way I thought fit: by laughing at myself and my situation – and admittedly allowing myself a lot more of the morphine!

It was nice to feel normal again. The last couple of weeks had been a strain and although I'd put a brave face on it all, I had felt it a bit of a burden to keep pace with my previous level of optimism. This was of course really stupid, because no one expected me or wanted me to be anything other than well again, irrelevant of how I dealt with the illness. Since defeating my inner demons the day before, however, I'd felt more centred again, and with Jonk and Jen popping round to watch the match like any friends might do made me feel a lot happier – well that and the morphine – and the cannabis – Oh! And the small French lagers I allowed myself to watch the match with.

Monday was the same as every Monday had been for the past month or so. I got up, put the plastic bag thing over my left arm to keep the PICC line and chemo bottle dry in the shower, and had some toast. Just because I felt better able to cope with the pain didn't mean that it went away, and toast is very low residue. I mentally braced myself before going to the loo, poured cold water down my bum whilst doing the doo-doo, and went to hospital.

Jane was there to take the mick out of me, which was always appreciated, whilst I moaned about how much it hurt when she pulled the plasters, and accompanying hairs, off my arms. Being treated normally by the hospital staff was very important; it made me feel that I was normal and not someone who should be pitied or cajoled just because I had cancer. Not that Rachel or my family did; they followed my lead and we just got on with it as best we could, which as I have mentioned, made my life a lot easier. From Jane's hair relocation program in Padgett Ward it was over to get nuked and home again – I had a good day.

Tuesday wasn't so good! One of the many downsides that can be caused by some strong painkillers is that they can constipate you; and whilst my weekend was good fun, I had used quite a lot of morphine. This I stopped on the Monday because I had a good day, in no small part owing to NOT going to the loo ten times. The result was Terrible Toilet Tuesday, which could have resulted in more morphine, but I realised the dangerous situation that this kind of cause and effect might create, and just poured lots of water over my arse during the course of the next couple of days. Come the Wednesday, the final day of my treatment, my insides had returned to their regular, if not predictable, selves and I was ready to be unplugged. First stop was Jane and all of the staff at Padgett Ward. I wanted to get them something as a thanks, but what do you get the people who have just helped save your life – not just in medical terms but in terms of support and, in Jane's case, mickey taking, which made me feel "normal"? I got the mandatory card and went for the tried and tested sweets option as the staff on the ward quite often had a tub of chocolates knocking around. I went for the wine gums and Jelly Babies option because it was still absurdly warm – they wouldn't melt – and well how can you go wrong with wine gums and Jelly Babies?

My schedule for the day was surprisingly compressed. My final radiotherapy session was pencilled in for 11 am, as opposed to 4 pm, before which I was off to see Jane, who was ready to unplug me from the bottle. I was initially quite taken aback by the matter-of-factness of the whole process; it was as if I was having an early dinner at a popular restaurant and being hurried through my dessert in order to accommodate the second sitting. These great people have to not only do an extraordinarily hard job, but they also have to be able to let people go after months of treatment without getting emotionally attached – that was all that I was witnessing. The end of one patient's treatment is followed by a hundred more, and whilst I had a good rapport with the nurses, that was it – no emotional farewells.

"When's your last radiotherapy session?" enquired Jane as she was unfixing the FU container from my PICC line.

"Later this morning. How long should I continue to have the PICC line attached? Another couple of weeks to be on the safe side, or leave it in should I need it up north?" When having the PICC line inserted I was very relaxed, mainly because I didn't know the details of insertion prior to the event, and therefore didn't have time to panic. I was all too aware this time that I had a thin tube reaching from my left elbow to just above my heart. On top of that, the hole where the pipe enters my skin had obviously healed around the pipe over the past few months and looking at it made me a tad jumpy.

"Nah! We'll pull it out when you're finished across at the Radiotherapy!"

"Cool!" I said, in as cool a way as I could muster – not the best time to turn into a big girl's blouse in front of the nurses, I thought. Shaking my head at my own wetness, I made my way over to the radiotherapy department for my final nuking session.

I'd had an amusing idea on the way to the hospital that day about how to commemorate my last visit to radiotherapy in London. The idea was simple really. As you know, when you have a cast on a broken bone it is always an excuse for people to sign it before it's removed. I obviously didn't have a cast on my bum, but I thought that it might be a bit of a giggle for the radiotherapy staff to all sign my arse and one of them to take a commemorative photo. This idea was pooh-poohed on from a great height by the staff nurse who said that no photos whatsoever could be taken within the radiotherapy room without the prior permission from the manufacturers of the equipment – trade secrets and all that, you know! I persevered, and suggested that we do a close-up of the signed arse and I didn't mind my "equipment" being photographed. Whilst I thought that this was a perfectly logical and well-formulated argument, the staff nurse had obviously been trained in the art of not changing your mind regardless of the validity of the argument, similar to the people skills training bestowed on club door staff, or bouncers if you prefer. I lost the "discussion" and had to make do with the usual thanks and handshakes, and with that done, bade my farewells and returned to Padgett to have the PICC line removed.

This time I was quite happy to sit at the back of the room and wait to be seen, being in no hurry to have a yard of tubing ripped from my arm. Jane came and got me and we went into a side room.

"This will only take a second and shouldn't hurt too much at all," said Jane reassuringly.

"Who's worried?" I lied, hopping onto the bed and proffering my left arm. "Didn't hurt going in so how bad could it be?" I added unconvincingly. I knew that I was being a wuss and tried to concentrate on the situation in hand. The pipe in my arm had to come out at some stage and now was as good a time as any.

"Ready?" asked Jane, taking the end in her right hand and putting her left on the inside of my left arm, just where the entry point was for the PICC line.

"This might tug a little to begin with!"

"Watch out for the skin that has grown over the hole!" I ventured, but Jane had already started to extract the tube. I felt the pull of the new skin around the PICC line lifting towards Jane before being torn and released. It didn't hurt at all and as Jane pulled this blue line out of my arm I started to laugh.

"What you laughing at – you weirdo?" She said, now using both hands to pull the line out in a hand over fist sort of manner.

"It's like the magic hanky trick that magicians do at birthday parties!"

"Wha ...?"

"You know. When they have a bit of a hanky sticking out from their fist or a small box and just keep pulling and pulling a never-ending procession of multicoloured hankies out from nowhere," I explained, as the last of the tube popped out of my arm leaving a small hole as a little reminder.

"You're not right – you!" Jane informed me, as she started to clean the wound and the surrounding area before applying a small plaster to cover the hole and prevent it from getting infected.

Leaving the side room, I went and found the other nurses who had been so kind to me over the past couple of months and thanked them all individually. Whilst I was obviously happy that the first part of my treatment was at an end, and that I wasn't going to have my arm hairs ripped from their follicles again, or be bombarded by radioactive particles, I was also very aware that the staff at Barts had, apart from Rachel et al., been the only people with whom I had had any meaningful contact with since leaving work. In a strange way the feeling was similar to that when as a kid you make friends on holiday, play 24/7 with them for a fortnight and then leave knowing that you wouldn't see them again. I gave Jane a hug and left feeling a little sad that I wouldn't be going back.

CHAPTER 21: GRAPE EXPECTATIONS

The first couple of weeks after the end of my treatment in London had passed by without much incident. I was still going to the loo eight to ten times a day, and the majority of the time it hurt to the point that I was having to brace my arms and almost lift myself off the toilet seat to avoid splitting any of my charred skin further. The radiotherapy had obviously had a significant effect on the internal workings of my plumbing and consequently I still had to be vigilant as to the needs of my bowel or bladder. When they wanted to be emptied there was none of this hold it till we get home malarkey; it was more of an internal Oy You! Toilet Now! Which, if nothing else, kept me on my toes – well, toilet if you want to be more accurate. It was strangely reassuring in the sense that I still had everything where it should be and all my bits were still working, albeit a little over enthusiastically.

As with a lot of things, time was a healer. Although I was still sore when coming up for my next appointment in Liverpool, my beleaguered butt was looking and feeling in considerably better condition than it had a couple of weeks previously. Rachel had decided that she wanted to come up for the weekend prior to my appointment with Dr Myint, to see my mum etc. Rachel had obviously been witness to the effects of the traditional chemo and radiotherapy, and it was natural that she wanted to get more involved. If just by being up north before the treatment made her feel more involved, as if that was possible, then so be it. We had decided that Rachel would come up on the Friday for the weekend prior to the MRI and check-up. This would allow me a couple of days of chilling with my family and more importantly give Mum and Rachel an opportunity to go shopping. I had already travelled up the week before, for my Dad's sixtieth birthday.

My appointment with Dr Myint had been put back till the 4th November owing to the overlap in treatment schedules between London and Liverpool. The plan was to assess whether or not the last twelve weeks of continual prodding, nuking, drugging and thermal pooing had been worth the considerable pain in the arse that it had turned out to be. If all were well, Dr Myint would recommend that I be put forward for the Papillon radiotherapy, which would be another step towards saving my arse – although quite how much of my arse would be left to save by that stage was a moot point. If not, it was the bag option (if that option was still available and the cancer hadn't spread) and, let's be realistic, that's still not as bad as the WORST CASE SCENARIO. So, whilst I was not getting my hopes up, I was approaching the next stage of treatment in a positive state of mind. Mum, on the other hand, was bouncing off the walls with anticipation and had no doubt that all would be good and that the Papillon was the way forward.

Before going to see Doctors Myint and Hershman first time round back in July, I'd had a CT scan to establish what was actually wrong with me. The scan had shown "floaty bits" in my lymphatic system back in July but the CT scans image hadn't been of sufficient quality to establish what they were. If these floaty bits turned out to be more than just an irregularity caused by the poor quality of the scan and were in fact malignant floaty bits, then my options would be severely reduced and drastic action would be needed. This, in conjunction with Dr Myint's need to have a new and more accurate picture of the current situation with the tumour, meant that I was to be scheduled for an MRI on November the 3rd. Owing to the rushed rearrangement of the check-up dates, I would be having my MRI at Arrow Park Hospital near Birkenhead in the north-west, which meant that I could add another hospital to my tour.

My rear had made continuous and encouraging improvement over the previous couple of weeks right up until the week before the appointment when I suddenly felt that something was amiss. I was fully tuned into my body's subtle nuances by this stage, and this new twinge from my "poo-hole" had me a tad concerned. Not that I thought it was linked to the tumour in any way, just that the sensation emitted was like a painful bruising, and that made going to the toilet even more uncomfortable. By the time Rachel had made her way up to Mum's in Chester on the Friday, the situation with my butt had got to the having to shift from one bum cheek to the other to avoid the painful feeling that would accompany sitting normally. I hadn't done this since the dark days of radiotherapy when the degree of burnt skin on my bits made sitting on the tube, travelling to and from the hospital, nearly impossible. This new sensation however was a combination of still- recovering cracked skin from the treatment, and a new pain emanating from just inside my bum hole. I had manually checked the affected area and there was nothing significantly wrong apart from what felt like a large spot right on the scorched skin around the entrance to my sphincter. It was like one of those spots that you get under the skin that will not develop into a squeezable head but just grows under the skin becoming bigger and tenderer.

On that Friday evening at Mum's we had dinner, and afterwards I lay prone on the couch to avoid putting undue pressure on my beleaguered bum. We discussed the upcoming events and the various scenarios that may or may not arise on Tuesday at the clinic with Dr Myint. Whilst I was confident that all would be well and that we would triumph in the end, I was keen to keep Mum on an even keel and to not get her any more excited than she already was. To move the conversation away from the upcoming check-up, I moved it onto the fact that at that moment there was very little chance of Dr Myint sticking anything up the dark side of my moon owing to a new and painful obstruction. It was agreed that if it was still bad the next morning we would try to get an appointment at the doctors for the Saturday afternoon to get it checked out. We also agreed that by the sounds of things it was probably just a pile, but it was worth getting a second opinion. Now, I have to be honest and say that up until that point in my life all that I knew about piles was from the pictures of blokes with a bunch of grapes hanging out of their arses scrawled on the walls of public toilets. I didn't really have a clue as to what they were and what they felt like, although I'd heard that they were painful at the best of times. So you can imagine what it must have felt like in my condition. I don't know about a bunch of grapes but it felt like someone had shoved a whole fruit basket up there.

Getting a doctors appointment, without being a psychic and knowing two weeks prior to being ill that you need one, is difficult at the best of times and at short notice is nigh on impossible. With this in mind, Mum found out where the local drop-in clinic was in Chester and when the best time would be to drop in. It turned out that mid afternoon was the optimum time so, with a bit of time to kill, we all went to Cheshire Oaks, an out of town retail centre, for a bit a retail therapy. I cannot lay the blame for this shopping venture solely at the feet of Mum and Rachel because when it comes to shopping I am definitely my mother's son. As I mentioned earlier, Mum is very stylish all the time, and since Mum clothed me from a young age, I have been a bit of a girl when it comes to shopping. Don't get me wrong: I don't mean that I try everything on then go back to the first shop – not at all. I power shop, know what I want and set my goals to find it. The problem arises when I don't have any specific clothing needs. I seem to gravitate towards shoes, boots and jackets. In fact, if it wasn't for the fact that I love boobs and don't fancy blokes I could be mistaken for being gay, I've got that many shoes and coats. On this trip however it was to kit Rachel out, so I wandered around whilst the ladies did their thing. Finishing off after lunch, Mum drove back into Chester, although I wasn't sure whether it was for me to go to the clinic or because M&S had a sale on.

"So where's the clinic?" I asked Mum

"It's easy – just go down there, over the bypass and it's up on the left after a couple hundred yards!"

"So you're not coming with me then?"

"Well, Marks and Sparks have a sale on and I thought that I would take Rachel and we'd go bargain hunting!"

"Oh! Well that's ... OK."

"We'll meet you at the Cross in an hour or so, or just ring when you're done and we'll meet you there. You'll be fine – go and have your pile looked at and we'll see you soon!" I was sure that I saw a smirk trying to break free across Mum's face but she held it together. Rachel just stayed out of the conversation and was probably more amused by the fact that I had just been well and truly told what was going to happen by my mum, as apposed to my painful walk as I minced off towards the drop-in centre. *Want to come to the treatment as long as it doesn't clash with shopping,* I thought darkly as I sort of walked off. Of course that wasn't true – there was no need for either of them to be sat with me in a waiting room for over an hour; it was just that, well, my bum really hurt.

The doctors' was as I expected: a long wait followed by five minutes of consultation. The doctor on duty at the drop-in centre was in his late forties to early fifties and was really nice about the whole thing, and was very careful when examining my new vineyard. He said that I had an accentuated pile and prescribed some cream to ease the pain and heal the affected area. He wished me luck with my upcoming treatment and with that I left to find how the shoppers had got on. When I first met Rachel she had about two pairs of shoes and a coat and that was it. I had done my bit, I felt, in showing her the basic principles of coordinating, accessorising and how to spot a bargain. Mum was a professional, however, and it was of no surprise to me that when I met up with them they had at least twelve bags between them.

"I have three tops, a skirt and a pair of trousers all for forty quid!" said Rachel in a manner that suggested she had just discovered religion. Mum had that "my work here is done" look about her and nodded in a sagely manner.

"Home?" said Mum, and with that we left – Rachel with a whole new world of opportunity ahead of her, Mum with a sense of a job well done, and me with my bum cream.

Arrow Park Hospital was a twenty minute drive from Mum's house and with the appointment for around ten in the morning we left a little early to avoid any commuter traffic. If the hospital was a little on the 1970s "we love concrete and right angles" side on the outside, the inside was a completely different proposition altogether. As you walked into the main entrance reception it was like walking into a shopping centre food hall. Gone are the days when a hospital's idea of in-house refreshment was some old dear from the WI selling week-old tea in paper cups for five pence a shout. There was everything from a W.H.Smith to buy your papers, to an open plan café selling everything from cappuccinos to croissants. I left Mum to her latte and cake whilst I went to find the MRI section and book myself in.

After following a number of signs down the wrong corridors like a rat in a labyrinth, I found the MRI check-in, completely void of patients and staff. After five minutes a receptionist appeared and pointed me down another corridor to the examination area itself where I had to go and re-check-in. An MRI is essentially a very accurate X-ray and stands for Magnetic Resonance Imaging. It basically works in the same way as a butcher's ham slicer, but instead of giving nice thin pieces of ham it looks at individual sections of your insides and gives thin pictures of the specific areas targeted. This requires the MRI machine to be located a little away from the main area, just like an X-ray ward, and is behind closed doors. I sat outside of the doors and waited for the next receptionist to appear to give me further instructions. A friendly, smiley face greeted me and offered me a clipboard with the standard hospital checklist on. You know, the "have you had this or have you ever suffered from that?" type of checklist. Also, because of the strength of the magnetic field within the MRI machine, they checked as to see whether I had any types of metal plates in my bones, false joints and even tattoos owing to the amount of lead in some ink.

"No, I'm additive free if you ignore the chemo etc.," I assured the nurse.

"Excellent. If you could just pop into that room over there and get changed into the gown provided; just leave your pants and shoes on."

"Doh!" I said looking down at my footwear.

Five minutes later I was sat outside the MRI room in my hospital gown and a subtle pair of Harley Davidson biker boots complete with metal badge on the ankle with the famous Eagle motif. I was mightily glad that I was the only person in the hall and that the nurses all had a good sense of humour. I was taken through the closed doors and introduced to the team, who again were lovely, and the process was explained to me. I was to be given a muscle relaxant to aid in the imaging of the area, and then I would be scanned for approximately forty-five minutes in the MRI machine itself. My primary concern was not the MRI – it was the muscle relaxant that I was to be given to aid with the scanning. I had already been to the loo, but I asked to go again and I tried to squeeze anything extra out of my plumbing prior to the scan, rather than the relaxant working rather too effectively, and me having a small accident on the examination table. Once satisfied that I was as empty as physically possible, I returned to the examination room leaving my boots outside.

The MRI room had a single machine in it with a sliding table protruding from the front. This would slide into a long tunnel, which ran through the entire width of the machine. It was like a larger fatter version of the CT doughnut, which I had been through at Homerton Hospital in London. The procedure was explained again with the added information about not moving a muscle when in the machine, and that I would be required to hold my breath for differing lengths of time during the scan. The machine was fairly loud which meant that I would be wearing headphones throughout the procedure so that I could hear the instructions from an adjacent control room. My only job was to pick the music to be played on the headphones for the duration of the scan. That done I was strapped onto the bed, a tap-needle was inserted into the back of my right hand, the drug was administered, and for once I was being inserted into a hole as opposed to the other way round.

I was glad at this stage that I had dropped a stone or so in weight over the previous few months because it was quite a snug fit. The ceiling of the MRI machine was no more than a foot above my face and my arms were pretty much flush to the tunnel walls; this would in all likelihood be a bit moody if you were claustrophobic.

"Can you hear me?" said the voice in my headphones.

"Yep! No probs."

"We're gonna start in a minute and the first session will last approximately four minutes," I was informed.

"Bit tight in here, isn't it? Imagine if you got excited – you'd be stuck in here for ages! Do you have a strictly no Viagra rule 24 hours prior to the MRI?" I enquired. Sniggering over the headphones made me feel a little better. I think it's always nice to know that the person working on you is on the same wavelength should there be any issues.

"OK, we're about to begin. Remember, don't move and should you need anything just say or press the emergency button. OK?"

"Yep!"

"Then we'll begin!" said the nurse who was in the control room. A wave of noise then flooded through the room as the machine started to work its magnetic magic. I had no idea that it was that noisy at all, not like these slick US medical dramas. This was a loud clacking noise, which I could only compare to Daffy Duck with a sinus complaint screaming in your ear. It went on for well over half an hour with the odd silent respite in between sessions, with me being called upon every now and then to hold my breath for thirty seconds or so. All in all there were no problems at all. Although a tight squeeze, the machine was relatively comfortable and the staff were marvellous. Should you ever have to have an MRI it is not as bad as some people make out; disconcerting – yes, noisy – definitely, but painful – not a bit. The table slid out, the tap in my hand was removed and I was helped off the bed and was back out and having a coffee with Mum after five minutes. Once done we went home to meet up with Rachel before she got the train back to London for work the next day, and for me to get ready for the meeting with Doctor Myint for the results so far.

The next morning we – Mum had invited herself along – arrived at Clatterbridge Hospital at around 10.30 am for my appointment with Doctor Myint. The purpose of this appointment was to assess whether the radiotherapy and chemo that had been administered in London had shrunk the tumour enough to be affected by any course of Papillon radiotherapy. I was considerably more concerned that Doctor Myint would want to either visually and/or in all likelihood manually check the tumour itself. The cream that I had received from the walk-in clinic was blatantly not designed for an embattled arse such as mine and had little effect, and I still was in a whole pile of pain. If you are still wondering why I should be concentrating on the granular issues surrounding the cancer and not the cancer itself, the reason was mental self-defence. I had no real fear that I was going to die. I had faith that the doctors were doing everything within their power to make that prediction come true, so panicking about the big things seemed pointless as they were taken care of. I was more concerned with the ongoing issues that were in my control or affected my immediate situation. So the possibility of having more radiotherapy was not as urgent a concern as the fact that I was about to have more back-port action, especially when said port was most certainly closed for business.

After the mandatory wait I was eventually called into Dr Myint's examination room. After a short while he appeared with a nurse and we started to discuss the treatment so far, and the various side-effects that I had encountered. We talked about the results from the MRI and how they showed that the combination of the radiotherapy and 5FU Chemo had significantly shrunk the tumour to a point where it was possible for me to be put forward for the Papillon radiotherapy, which would hopefully finish the job enough to allow surgery. We chatted for about ten minutes and to be honest I had thought that I had got away without being impaled but:

"Before I let you go I want to take a quick look at the area myself!"

"Wha …?"

"If you could just pop up on the bed and pull your trousers down with your bum hanging over the edge for me!"

"To be honest I'd rather not. My arse is still burnt from being nuked and now there's a soddin' great pile up there too!"

"I don't really care; I still have to look," replied Dr Myint. The "don't care" was a mistake. Now I was annoyed, and felt it was my duty to point that out to him.

"Well, how about you go and have thirty-odd nuking sessions and then I'll shove that lightsaber up your soddin' arse. See how you feel!" I was a tad peeved, to say the least. "Why can't I just wait a week or so, and someone at Barts could have a butchers and let you know?" This seemed like a logical suggestion to me: one NHS, one goal – my hole. No probs.

"Fine. Then it will cost you about £500 to have the check-up if that is what you want, but they may just decide that the risk is too great and insist on the full treatment and the stoma." Like a lot of professionals, Dr Myint is very "professional" and his reaction to some layman disagreeing with him was to immediately shut up shop and retreat to "it's my ball and I'm taking it home" position. This meant that I had two choices: either pay a load of money that I couldn't afford and possibly lose the chance of having this treatment or be examined and be in some major discomfort. I was fully aware that Dr Myint's only concern was my long-term well-being and was truly looking after my best interests but, well, it was gonna hurt – a lot. I turned to look Dr Myint squarely in the eye and tried to read his thoughts. The nurse just stood quietly and nervously out of the way like someone waiting for a mega firework to go off.

"Fine. But I want lots of lube!" And with that I dropped my pants got on the bed and puckered up.

With the examination done, Mum was called in to hear the news that I would be clear to go forward to the next stage, the Papillon radiotherapy. Mum had heard some growling from the waiting room and could see from my face that I had been annoyed – a kind of "post-fucked-off glow" if you like, but Dr Myint just said that all was well after some initial silliness. I took that as it was meant – no harm, no foul – gave him a nod in recognition and left, only to be grilled by Mum as to what had happened on the way home.

The important thing was that, all silliness aside, I had been accepted to go on to the next stage of the treatment – two separate overnight stays on the 10th and 11th and the 24th and 25th of November. That would hopefully save my arse.

Note to doctors – the reason for my outburst was a simple one. Whilst you might be onto your tenth arse, cervix, ear, eye, nose or throat of the day it will have been the patient's first impaling or whatever, of the day. Remember that there is a person at the end of your finger, lightsaber, etc. and they are probably a little nervous and random buggering can ruin an otherwise fine morning!

CHAPTER 22: THE BUTTERFLY EFFECT

Papillon radiotherapy is an important development in the battle against colon/rectal or lower bowel cancer. The procedure is designed to administer low-level radiation directly to the tumour or area affected, therefore limiting (hopefully) the collateral damage that can occur during the traditional wide-beam treatment – i.e. a crispy arse etc. There are two main reasons why your doctor, if they have even heard of this treatment, would recommend Papillon assuming that the cancer hasn't spread:

1) They feel that you are not fit enough to go through with a full operation and that you are a high anaesthetic risk.

2) You do not want any surgery that involves either a permanent or temporary stoma – that's bag to you and me.

Not all bowel cancers, as I have already mentioned, are going to be helped by this treatment or are suitable for local treatment. There is a marginally higher risk of local recurrence – 10% as opposed to 2 –4% with the traditional treatment – and should this happen you will have to go through with the whole bag option. The greatest risk of this recurrence is within the first three years after treatment.

The goal of this treatment from my point of view was to kill as much of the cancer as possible to enable me to qualify for the TEM surgery. The way I looked at it was simple: should this work – cool – I've still got a bum and should it not work – well at least I will have tried and still will end up with the stoma or – as I liked to call it by then – a "bum bag". The details of how this treatment was going to be administered had as yet to be disclosed. All that I knew was that I would be going in, staying overnight, being nuked and coming home. How bad could that be?

Once again I came up from London a couple of days prior to the hospital appointment so that I could be at home for Mum's birthday as well as doing the rounds of family and friends. Aside from that I was trying not to go out of my head with boredom. One of the ways I dealt with various bits of me falling apart or off completely during the treatment was to immerse myself in little routines. I would get up, shower with the bread bag thingy on, have breakfast, and go for a walk – carefully – kill a couple of Dark Jedi's on the Xbox and then off to the hospital. Now that the treatment had finished I felt as if I was a bit of an oxygen thief to be honest. Don't get me wrong – from any point of view I was still extremely ill, but, man, was I bored or what? Mum had by this time taken medical leave from work owing to the understandable stress of having your child be treated for cancer. So Mum was at home all the time, which meant that we would, and often did, just hop, gingerly, into the car and bugger off for the day – which was nice!

There was something that caught my eye this time round that I had either missed or hadn't been there upon my last visit to Mum's – Get Well cards.

As I have said several times in this book, it was my family, Rachel and friends whom I felt most sorry for, not myself. *Having* is a lot easier than watching! Mum had left work owing to stress and, to some extent, depression. Never shown in front of me, of course, but it must have been obvious to her friends and colleagues. The lounge was awash with cards, flowers and good luck messages, all of which were for Mum. It was at this point I realised that I hadn't received a single card, not an email, not a dickey-bird. The company that I had worked for and had been a franchise owner for, for over seven years, had not even rung me to see how the treatment was going. The vast majority of my so-called work friends had not been in contact since the last time I had been into the office and, yes, I hadn't really cared right up until I saw evidence of all of Mum's.

"Who's all these for? Who's the sick one here?" I said with feigned hurt.

"Nice aren't they? Just from work and friends there's one here for you. Well it's not really a card but you had a prayer said for you at their local church."

"Aww, that's nice – not that I'm a believer but at this stage I'll take all the help I can get," I replied with genuine gratitude. I found it strange that a woman I had probably never met cared enough to do that, but people I had known for years couldn't be arsed (no pun intended) to even ring!

"I know why I haven't got any cards – it's because they don't know what to say," I declared, in a eureka type manner for added effect. Mum just waited for the stream of bollocks that was sure to accompany such an outburst.

"No, really, bear with me." I exclaimed. "If you get a cold or have a broken leg then chances are that you will 'Get Well Soon'; what do you say to someone who has cancer? Don't die yet?"

"Oh Mark! Behave." Mum was trying hard not to smile too much and just ended up with a toothy smirk breaking out across her face.

"I think I'm on to something here. Don't Die Yet cards – recyclable of course just in case you do, obviously."

"MARK!!"

"Sorry, but come on. I can't believe you got all these and I got bugger all; that's just not cricket if you ask me." Mum just nodded and hmmed a little.

"Beer?"

"Love one!" And with that I was done.

Clatterbridge Hospital was not a complete stranger to me; I had spent a bit of time there when I was younger (another story for another time). Nevertheless, going in overnight felt like a slight escalation of my situation. It wasn't, of course, that the wide-beam radiotherapy and chemo that I had already received was considerably less dangerous than Papillon, but the whole going in thing made it feel more important.

The Clatterbridge Centre of Oncology (CCO) is a very nice hospital. It is clean, new, and spacious, all in all not the Victorian abattoir type scenario we are all used to seeing on the news. This is a nice shiny one. I was shown through to the ward, introduced to the staff nurses and shown to my bed. This was an open ward with partitions separating groups of four to six beds and of course the ladies' ward. There were three other guys in my little section and once again I was the youngest by a good fifteen to twenty years. I introduced myself to the chaps and settled in, unpacked my overnight bag and had a little wander round to find the all-important loos. Once done, I cracked open a new book and made myself comfy. It was only early afternoon and I was due for a couple of visits from staff nurses and doctors over the next couple of hours, to go over what the plan of action would be.

I ended up chatting to a sixty-year-old guy in the next bed. He was also in for colon/bowel cancer and had nothing but positive things to say about the treatment that he had so far received. We did however talk about pain relief and what drugs we had used and what works and what doesn't.

"I've just started to smoke cannabis!" he declared. "At the age of sixty! Doesn't 'alf help ya know!"

"I'm with you on that one," I agreed. "The amount of drugs that I should have been on and none of them really worked. Ok, smoking isn't really the way forward when you've got cancer but needs must."

"Takes the edge off," he agreed. "Just sort of … levels off the pain. If you need some just let me know!" he offered.

"Thanks, but I'm based in London. Know what ya mean though – brings you down to a manageable plateau without wiping you out completely." I had found my first ally; now I felt at home.

A nurse came over eventually to go through the agenda for the next twenty-four hours, which included two enemas – oh joy; one that evening around nine and then one the next morning a couple of hours before the treatment. A porter would be collecting me and taking me down to the treatment area, after which I could go home a couple of hours later – no probs! With the ground rules established I decided to explore the ward a little more, find the TV room and generally be nosey. I had slipped into something more comfy by this time – the sarong – and just pottered about. This is where I started to understand a little more about the seriousness of this disease. I met a gent – we'll call him Frank – in the TV room, who had cancer of the throat. When I was being nuked back in London, what I didn't mention was the array of masks and ceramic/plastic covers that they had in the bunker for the different types of cancer. Face masks, boob covers, etc. that would protect the unaffected areas of the body from the damaging effects of the wide-beam radiotherapy. I think something akin to a cricket box could definitely be a winner for arse cancer if you ask me, not that anyone did.

Frank's face was a tale of two halves. While being treated he obviously had to wear a Phantom of the Opera half mask. The top half of his face was pretty much OK; however, from the base of his nose down it was not so good. You remember how I tried to convey the degree of burning to my rear towards the end of my treatment; well, this was Frank's lower face and throat. His skin was burnt red raw, he had limited lateral movement of his head, tubes emanating from his nostrils which were attached to a wheelie machine that fed him. All in all, a mess! I don't know how old he was – I'd guess late sixties – but I imagine this wasn't how he had envisaged his dotage and once again I felt very, very fortunate. As I walked into the TV room he rotated his upper torso to be able to look at who was coming in, and I was met with sad, but strong, watery blue eyes. I am able to make light of just about any situation, but this guy's situation was well beyond that. I simply offered my hand, introduced myself and asked if he needed anything. He was waiting to see if the England friendly was on terrestrial TV that night. To be honest, all the conversational details with Frank haven't really registered in my memory. I just remember talking to him very briefly and the pain it caused him to just do that. After a short while a nurse popped her head in the room and with an "Oh so there you are!" and informed me that it was enema time. I bade my farewells and Frank responded with a slight tilt of the head and a single bat of his weary eyelids.

The time was now around nine in the evening. The point of the evening and morning enemas were to clear me out; this would enable Dr Myint to see the problem area more clearly, and therefore execute a more accurate positioning of the radiotherapy machine. Now, the only enema that I had experienced up until that point was the DIY mushroom jobbie at the Royal Liverpool prior to being impaled by the hand-held harpoon gun posing as an ultrasound scanner. This session had two sachets, each about the size of a bag of Skittles with a small tube at the end (no prizes for guessing where that was going), and was to be administered by the nurse. The curtain was pulled round the bed and the nurse instructed me on what was going to happen.

"I'm going to insert the tube and empty the contents of both sachets. Now what I need you to do is to try to hold the liquid in for as long as possible before going to the loo – do you think you can do that for me Mark?"

"Empty sachets, hold it in and bum gargle for as long as possible, before going to the loo – got it!" I confirmed. I'd gotten quite used to this whole hospital malarkey by now so was pretty confident that I could cope.

"Just roll onto your left side and … nice skirt!"

"Sarong, Thanks! Our Ben got it in Indonesia and let me have it, which was nice." I corrected.

"Just roll onto your left side, pull up your *sarong* and lift your knees up to your chest. Ready?" It's a strange sensation having liquid pumped up your bum – cold at first and then nothing.

"All done; try to keep it in as long as possi … " I was up and off – holding it in was not an option. Sprinting with clenched butt cheeks was a bit of a forte of mine by now, and I was bloody glad that it was otherwise I would have left one hell of a nasty snail trail. I made it into the toilet, pulled up me skirt and dropped, whilst what felt like the entire contents of my stomach – kidneys 'n' all – evacuated.

"OHHH! MYYY! GODDD!" I cried as I was wracked by wave after tsunami strength wave of liquid hell erupting from my arse. You know when people say things like "tastes like burnt rubber", that they have obviously never dined on that particular delicacy but you can sympathise with their position? Well, this felt like my arse was gargling with pure lemon juice, with a touch of nitro-glycerine and a splash of bleach. It was not good! I was bent double as my bowel tried desperately to expel this alien liquid. I had a right sweat on I can tell you. The first ten minutes were the worst, but the whole experience lasted about twenty-five minutes at least, and my stomach felt like it had been wrung empty. I staggered out of the toilet, glistening with sweat. I looked something like Jim Carrey did in *Ace Ventura* when he came out of the toilet after battling a shark. Framed by the toilet door I looked at the nurse, who had stopped whatever she was doing after seeing this shell of a man emerge from the loo, and I could only waft my arm behind me and quote the great man himself – "You *Do Not* want to go in there!" Then I turned and staggered off to have a little lie-down.

As I have mentioned, I'm not the greatest sleeper in the world. Now, considering that hospitals are places where the sick are supposed to rest and recuperate, I feel that they are not really holding up that end of their job description. Firstly I was in an open ward, quite a nice one admittedly, but old people make all sorts of weird noises when they sleep. The lights are never off completely, for obvious reasons but still! As all those who, like me, suffer with insomnia will testify, the best sleeping time is around four to six in the morning. I was woken at 5.30 with a cheery "Morning pet – fancy a cuppa?" by a nice lady with a very noisy tea trolley. I'm not the most compos mentis person at that time in the morning, especially with no more than an hour's sleep, so I thought I handled myself quite well considering.

"Thanks – white and a small sugar – wait. No. Is it tea or coffee? Err. What?" I garbled still with only one of my eyes having realised that I was awake.

"Whatever you want dear!" She was obviously used to patients having mental lead time issues when it's still *bloody dark outside*.

"Err, umm … coffee please!" I managed as second eye and brain caught up.

"What time is it?"

"Just gone half five dear; there you go."

"Wha … Cheers."

As I accepted the warm dark liquid – coffee was a bit of a strong word for it to be honest – the morning staff nurse appeared and was considerably more forthright, informing me that once I had finished the "coffee" I should go and shower before having breakfast. I acknowledged her with a baleful glare in best Paddington Bear tradition, and finished the drink. Post-shower, I declined breakfast knowing full well that around nine that morning I would be flushed out again by Satan's groin sweat and the thought of having any solid matter within the vicinity of my colon just didn't bear thinking about.

Sure enough at around nine the nurse turned up with the enema and the curtain was again closed around my bed. This time, however, I was prepared. Not that I could change the effect or the sensation, but I remembered to grab my book as I pelted off towards the bog with the words of the nurses ringing in my ears: "Try to hold it in for as long as possible." Yeah right! This dose wanted out more than the alien in John Hurt's chest. Once the initial ooing and arrghing had passed, I got on with reading my book whilst trying to stop losing all sensation in my legs owing to the intensity and prolonged nature of the toilet action. "This is just the preparation, the appetizer, I'entrée," kept going through my head as I removed myself from the loo with an audible "thwup", not too dissimilar to the noise made when you open a Tupperware container, and then back to my bed.

The clock ticked slowly towards 11 am and my rendezvous with Dr Myint and his new nuking contraption. Sure enough, just prior to eleven a lady porter turned up with a wheelchair to take me to the treatment room. I had already gone commando under my sarong, so as to aid access, and was as prepared as I was likely to be. I had no jitters about the procedure, because again I didn't really know what was going to happen, and bottom line it was hopefully going to aid me in my quest. I got into the chair and allowed myself to be wheeled off to the treatment room, although I felt a bit of a slacker allowing a lady to push me – my nana would have had a fit! After a couple of minutes we arrived at our destination with Dr Myint and a couple of radiographers waiting outside a small room for me. I thanked the porter and waited to be told what was going to happen and where to go. I was introduced to the team and the mandatory "new guy" who was observing the procedure for the first time.

I was informed that the treatment was going to take about five minutes, although I would be required to be in the room for up to half an hour as the positioning of the treatment machine was of utmost importance. The reason for this is that the low energy X-rays are directly applied to the area where the tumour is, and will only be penetrating a few millimetres. As I mentioned, this means that the surrounding healthy tissue isn't affected, unlike the blanket bombing technique of the traditional wide-beam radiotherapy. Oh! And it might be a bit uncomfortable.

With my debrief out of the way I was led through to the treatment room by the radiographer, followed by Dr Myint. The room was very small and was full of various contraptions and trolleys brimming with impaling equipment, the modern version of Frankenstein's laboratory. In the centre of the room was a trolley bed that looked as if it had been in a car accident. About a third of the way along the bed it was crumpled up like a mini gym-horse had been placed under the sheet; it was over this that I was going to have to kneel and present my derrière. This was obviously asking for trouble in the same way as Oliver proffering his bowl to Mr Bumble, although more was not what I wanted. I looked at the bed, back at Dr Myint and back to the bed again and shook my head with an air of resignation that things were going to go all a bit Pete Tong for my poor bum.

"If you could just get up on the bed and bend over the treatment board with your legs against it as much as possible please!" said the radiographer. I looked at Dr Myint and shook my head again; this was going to be bad and I knew it. Dr Myint knew that I knew it, and, importantly, that I knew that he knew that I knew. He averted his gaze for a moment so as not to see the look of pleading upon my face. I clambered onto the bed, bent over the gym-horse with all of the enthusiasm of a man choosing the type of rope he was about to be hanged with, and tried to make myself comfortable.

"First we must find were the tumour is!" said Dr Myint.

"Up me arse!" I offered helpfully.

"Hmmm" was all I got as the radiographer wheeled over a trolley with medical equipment on it, including Dr Myint's trusty lightsaber. It was like a torture scene in a movie. I have to add that the machine, which was obviously going to be inserted into my nether regions at some stage, did look incredibly like the laser that was about to bisect 007 in Goldfinger. I felt like Bond: do you expect me talk? No Mr Bond. I expect you to die. Except with added lube.

Lube was applied and the sigmoidoscope was inserted and then, to enhance the greater good and educate those who needed to know, was offered to all an' sundry to have a look. I looked back over my shoulder to see if they had started to invite random members of the public in to have a look when the radiography nurse asked if I was OK. The look I gave her might well have melted lead but at least she asked. Once the sigmoidoscope was removed, Dr Myint enquired as to how I was and informed me that he was going to apply some local anaesthetic cream – bum Bongella – before inserting the treatment tube. Now, I don't know about you, but what mental pictures does "treatment tube" conjure in your mind? Maybe one of those thin jobbies that you see on hospital dramas – the type that is put down a patient's throat to aid breathing perhaps? Not on your Nelly! It looked for all the world like a cross between the Sputnik space probe and a funnel you use to pour oil into your car. The crowning glory of this technical monstrosity was the shiny chrome dildo that Dr Myint was holding in his other hand – *the applicator.* The applicator was about the length and width of a Monty Cristo No.1 cigar and was very shiny indeed. The end was bullet shaped to ease entry and was inserted into the open end of the Sputnik/funnel device before coming to rest in the tube end of the treatment tube. This was then inserted; the idea being that the applicator would help insertion, and then would be removed leaving Sputnik protruding like some sort of desert dew collector from my arse. It needed more than a bloody chrome dildo to ease the entry of this device – it needed a litre of Jack Daniels, a bottle of poppers and a shoehorn, I can tell ya.

"What the f … ?"

"Its OK – just try to keep as still as possible," said the nurse.

"Well I can hardly go anywhere can I? Sunny, mate, that's just not good … at all!" I strained. My hands made fists in the sheets and I started to semi-raise myself onto my elbows to try to improve the angle of entry, all to no avail.

Then once it was in, I had to be manoeuvred into position to line up the funnel/bum hole and the arm of the treatment machine down which the X-rays would be poured. This involved the treatment table being manually wheeled about until there was a snug fit. This was now taking the piss, as far I was concerned. Not only was my butt well and truly plugged and beginning to feel the strain but all the extra movement of Sputnik, caused by trying to attach the treatment machine, was beginning to chafe somewhat – Houston we definitely have a problem! In terms of butt stretch, think putting your fist into your mouth and then typing out the alphabet on a large keypad with that elbow.

Eventually, I was attached and the room was evacuated, leaving me trussed like a pig that was prepared by a short-sighted chef, with the apple in the wrong end. A small curtain was pulled back on the adjacent wall to reveal a small window through which I could see the faces of the observing crowd. It felt a little like one of those black and white documentaries of the original nuclear tests, with white gown clad scientists hiding in a bunker waiting to see what would happen when they pressed the big red button. Unfortunately for me, the nuke was lodged up my arse. The treatment started and as with the other radiotherapy treatment I didn't or couldn't feel a thing. What I *could* feel was my arse getting really annoyed with this strange contraption being where it blatantly shouldn't be, and the increase in strain that this was exerting. After a couple of minutes the treatment finished, and Dr Myint et al. re-entered the room.

"Get this thing out of my arse – now!"

"In a moment! We just have to disconnect the treatment machine. Are you OK?" said the radiography nurse.

"What do you think? I've just had Sputnik crash-land up my arse and radiation poured into the opening. No my arse is definitely not OK!" Not her fault, I know, but stupid question.

Dr Myint just told me to put my clothes back on and wait outside for a moment. This I did, walking like a man who had accidentally backed onto a charging rhino. After a couple of minutes Dr Myint emerged from the treatment room followed by his team. I don't know if the couple of minutes were used to check the apparatus or to allow me to calm down enough to not risk physical injury. Either way Dr Myint was happy with the way the treatment had gone and said that I could go home in an hour or so once I had recovered. The porter re-appeared and offered me the chair; I waved her away; this time I was definitely walking – sitting down was the last thing that I wanted to do at that moment in time. Once I was back to my bed, I rang Mum to come and get me and was out of there within an hour of the treatment.

"So how was it?" asked Mum enthusiastically. I just looked at her. "Oh! Not good then!"

"Just get me home and I'll tell you everything." And with that we headed off, secure in the knowledge that there would be another visit to my Moon Base Alpha in a fortnight's time.

CHAPTER 23: HOLE IN MY POCKET

Once again, I returned to London for the interim period between treatments. With the start of the Papillon treatment came the realisation that there was a fair chance that I would not be back to work early in the New Year. This meant that I had to attend to the financial realities of having cancer and being self-employed. One of the best things about having a small business is that when it's good it's great, but the flip side is when it's crap it's very crap. I had managed to save a little from the business but not enough to allow me to be financially independent, for say the next six months or so. Like most of us who have loans or credit cards I had cover for illness and unemployment, and with all an' sundry getting benefits in London even if they are not supposed to be here, I thought that it would be straightforward to get my house in order. Wrong!

I rang my local council in London, and apprised them of the situation and they sent me out the forms to fill in. I am a reasonably intelligent guy, but these forms are unbelievable. I know there is a whole cottage – well, terrace/flat – industry in this country built up around lying on these forms and never having to work, pay bills or be responsible for anything your entire life. Unfortunately, should you have made an effort in life, had no links with the Taliban, be heterosexual and dare I say it English with a job, you are fucked. A sympathetic jobcentre worker later informed me that my biggest mistake was to tell the truth on the forms. The process went like this: I sent the forms, they lost the forms. After a period of time I reapplied. They lost those, I tried again, having moved by this time – same district – and they wanted proof of things like I had cancer. They got it; they wanted proof of no income and they got that. They wanted me to prove that I wasn't working – same as last question? I pointed out that I had cancer and had spent the intervening months being poked, prodded, drugged and nuked. Then they wanted all the information again and again and again.

To say that the system is a mess is being kind; I don't know if it's a race thing, a class thing or government guidelines on the processes of qualification and the hiring of absolute muppets who barely speak English (not all of the staff; a lot were good people who were just as sorry and frustrated for me as I was for myself). I can tell you that I had bailiff notices from the council tax people, who were the very ones who were taking so long to sort my claim in the first place. *I can't give you money that you haven't given me yet* – was my point to them! I think if we don't get paid on time or at all, we should be allowed to send them a nasty letter saying that we are coming down the social to take computers equalling the value of the money that they owe us. Just to let you know, bearing in mind I had no income, no sick pay (self-employed), no job to go back to (closed company down) and was living in London (Rachel could afford to pay half the rent etc. but wasn't on enough to shoulder the whole lot, nor should she have had to!) and I applied for benefit in Oct/Nov 2003, I received my first pound of housing and council tax benefit in August 2005 only after threatening to write to my local MP.

OK! Local government – pile of ... well you get the picture, but surely the big financial institutions would be better. I had several bits and bobs hanging around with various banks etc. and let them know of the situation. Student Loans, after initial umming and arring, were good and just wanted to be kept up to date with my progress. Egg Finance, with which I had a couple of cards, although I had no cover, were wonderful. They listened, offered alternatives and acted upon them promptly. Although I was not working, they gave me the option to take a small £5,000 loan to consolidate my various cards and leave me with extra cash as well as a pay break for 3 months – very good and friendly staff. HSBC had passed an old student loan to a third party claims company who set a nasty little pit bull of a phone loan harasser on me. I explained that I did not have a job owing to the fact that I had cancer and could I put off payment for a couple of months. His answer was that he didn't care that I had cancer and would send bailiffs round should I not pay up. This information I passed on to the public relations department of HSBC and they were very quick and apologetic about the behaviour of their contractors and we agreed a settlement plan to pay off the loan, which I did. I always pay my debts and all I wanted was my present circumstances taken into account and some time to pay.

Halifax, on the other hand, was nearly as slow, stupid and pig-headed as the council. Of all of the loans I had this was the smallest, about £1,500, and Halifax were the one company that I thought would be fairly straightforward. I had cover on the loan, I had been a customer for over ten years and I had cash and tracker ISAs with them, and so I was confident. It started as usual with me sending in a letter from the doctors saying that I was under treatment for colon cancer. They then wanted previous payslips to prove that I was working and a letter from my accountant stating that the company had been suspended and was in the process of being closed and that I was not taking any money from it. This was done and I thought that would be that; I would have a break until I regained work at the very least, maybe even the loan cancelled, as it was so small. Oh no!

One of the good things about being self-employed is that you can wait until you have earned enough in the financial year before you start to pay National Insurance. Business hadn't been great for a lot of 2003 and so I was taking a small wage in order to keep as much money in the business as possible. After a couple of months I got a reply saying that I didn't qualify because I did not pay National Insurance. What? This I passed onto my accountants who sent me all of the 2002/2003 tax receipts and payslips with a confirmation letter of my tax status. No help. Apparently in the minuscule print there was something about paying National Insurance. I pointed out that I was claiming on critical illness cover and not unemployment, but still got the no hope answer. Have you read the book or seen the film by John Grisham called *The Rainmaker*, where the phone people of the insurance company are told to deny all claims straight off to delay or put off the prospective claimant? Whilst I'm not suggesting that this is what actually happens, it is what this felt like. You have cover, which they encourage you to pay saying "what if you get ill or lose your job?" Then when you get ill and lose your job they throw some small print bollocks at you. This meant that although I had zero income or benefit I was having to pay half of all of the bills, rent, council tax *and* £100 or so a month to a bank that I had paid extra to, to be protected.

The claim went on until August 2004, by which time I had resorted to throwing logic at them. I eventually managed to find an internal champion on the phone that actually listened as opposed to just saying no. I pointed out, again, that the reason that no tax had been paid was that, being self-employed, I only pay NI once I have earnt enough money; therefore should I have been diagnosed say in September I would have qualified because I would have started to pay NI. Basically I said: "Are you saying that I got cancer at the wrong time of year for Halifax bank?" to which they did the old *that's not what we're saying*. It *was*. My guy on the inside pointed out to someone that the whole NI thing was bollocks because I was claiming under critical illness not unemployment. Nearly twelve months. Unbelievable!

I apologise for bringing a whole lot of financial realism into the book but to be honest I was planning on living and had to be responsible for my bills and loans. Money is one of those things that can be forgotten when you are being subjected to serious medication and treatments. Battling pencil pushers as well as cancer is the last thing that you want to be dealing with. The cancer is often easier because at least you know what you're dealing with. As for everyone else they will just sit around and let you die before actually being arsed to help. Make provision for muppets and get onto any outstanding debts straight away. If you are self-employed and have certain banks giving you a loan – check the small print or get cancer at a more convenient time for them.

CHAPTER 24: THE POWER OF ONE

After the break, I returned to the north-west for the second session of Papillon and the final leg of nearly four months of treatment. I had experienced some of the greatest pain and funniest moments of my life since starting chemo and radiotherapy and it was this thought that I kept in my mind and heart as I readied myself. The tumour had shrunk and the treatment had been going to plan but there was still no guarantee that even after all of the nuking and drugs, I would be able to have the operation to save my arse. I was still as positive as the day that I got the news that I had cancer, if not more so, having met and been treated by so many wonderful, clever and kind people. The reality was that it was a long shot that a tumour of the size and depth of mine could, let alone should, be treated. The journey had become the goal as much, if not more than, the outcome.

Throughout the treatment I had maintained, for my own mental stability, that I was not as ill as some that I had met. The next session of Papillon was again a two-day one-night escapade, during which I would be dosed in the evening and morning before having a Titan missile inserted into my rear launch shoot. I had no sleep the last time I was in and thought that it would save a bed and my sanity if I could pop in, get dosed – spend some quality time with the toilet – then go home and return in the morning refreshed and ready for impaling! This idea I pitched to Doctor Myint and after some deliberation he said that he couldn't see any problem as long as I was at the hospital for 6 pm (enema was at nine as per) and had to stay at least an hour before going home. Mum dropped me off and I made my way to the ward and was shown to my bed. There were some new faces this time around, and me being me, I had soon introduced myself and struck up some conversation. One guy who was pretty young – early to mid forties – was also in for the Papillon, although his situation was different and, to me, even more disturbing. He had come over from the north-east, proving that you don't need psychic family friends to find out about Papillon – just a clued-up GP and Google. He didn't even have cancer. Let me explain! This poor guy had gone to the doctors with similar symptoms to myself, probably without the aid of Chinese food, however, and had discovered that he had a polyp in his colon.

Polyps are growths, which develop in the colon as well as other parts of the body. They vary in size and appearance. They may look like a wart when small and like a cherry on a stem when they grow. They can with time turn into cancer; although polyps of the colon and rectum are almost always benign they can cause painless rectal bleeding. There may be single or multiple polyps. The incidence of polyps increases with age. The cumulative risk of cancer developing in an unremoved polyp is 2.5% at 5 years, 8% at 10 years, and 24% at 20 years after the diagnosis. You are almost four times less likely to get cancer if you have them removed and as with all things cancerous your individual and historic situation will affect the outcome and diagnosis.

The problem was not the polyp; it was the fact that he had decided to get it sorted and not "hope for the best". He had done the right thing, for him, and had opted to get it removed regardless as to whether it was cancerous or not. The problem was that the surgeon had managed to not remove all of the polyp and owing to the scar tissue nobody could safely tell whether or not the little bit left was malignant or not – so they had suggested the bag. "You have got to be having a laugh?" was all I could manage. I, at least, knew that I would die should I not do something. This poor sod had done the right thing as far as he was concerned, and could lose his arse just because some "arsehole" was arsing around when they should have been concentrating – if you know what I mean.

Papillon had come to the rescue because of the non-evasive nature of the treatment. It was hoped that the area around the polyp could be treated and he and his arse could live happily ever after. I was astonished not only at the auto response that he should blithely have his butt hole removed but the fact that he was quite calm about it – I would have been spitting chips I tell ya.

Later that evening, prior to the enema, I popped into the TV room to see who was about and what was on the box, when I bumped into Frank. He was dressed in slacks and a shirt with a collar, stood in the centre of the TV room struggling with his top buttons and tie. "You look very smart" I commented. "Are they letting you out for a few days?" His watery eyes moved to meet mine as I walked around to face him, still unable to properly move his head owing to the burns of the radiotherapy treatment. Smiling as much as he physically could when he saw me, the minimal shake of his head barely distinguishable, he rasped that his wife was coming to visit and could I help him with his top button and tie. This is what I mean when I talk about not worrying about my situation and being humbled by the strength of those others with cancer who I have had the privilege to meet. This gentleman's face was half burnt off. Most of us would be hard pushed to get out of bed and dress ourselves at all but here he was making an effort for the woman he loved to show her that he was all right and that little things like not being able to eat solids, talk or move his head would not allow him to lower his personal standards. In today's Britain we are almost constantly told that being British is bad, we should be ashamed of our history and we should be like everyone else – well, bollocks to that. This man's strength and courage was a wonder to behold, and that sense of propriety and personal pride is what made our country great, and I was proud for the first time in a long time to be British.

Silently and very carefully I did up his top buttons leaving the very top one, although he hadn't wanted me to, because of the sheer distress it would have caused to his already red raw skin. I tied his tie in a double Windsor and he nodded his thanks. "You look great," I said trying to control the emotion in my voice. "She'll be very proud of you and I'm sure at this rate you'll be out of here in no time!" Again, a small curt nod and single blink of his weary eyelids to convey his thanks accompanied by a brief painful smile. We both knew that the chance of recovery was slim to none but that didn't stop him being one of the most inspiring people I have ever met. I briefly clasped both his shoulders with my hands and left him to straighten his tie and organise his food and water tubes that were still protruding from his nose so that they too would be tidy for when his beloved arrived. I went back to my bed, pulled the curtain around and had a little sob, as much for this wonderful man and his partner, as for those who are never ever going to understand that there is more to life than their own selfish desires and unimportant gripes. As for me, well I had two enemas and a nuking session to be getting on with, none of which felt as important or scary as they had a couple of minutes previously.

CHAPTER 25: PAPILLON PART DEUX

Nine o'clock on the dot and the nurse arrived holding the two bags full of the enema.

"I've had a cunning plan!" I declared as she began to pull the curtain round the bed.

"Hmmm!"

"Well, whilst I know that you're gonna give me the enema regardless of what I say, I am taking up one of only two toilets on the ward for a good half an hour or so. Are there any spare rooms where I can be dosed and keep out of everyone's way?" I thought that this was a reasonable request in light of the fact that (a) the majority of the ward was old and bladder or bowel control was not a recognised forte of my fellow patients, and (b) well, you know what it's like having a poo in a public toilet be it a bar, hotel, train station whatever; it's quite hard to concentrate on the job at hand, and you try to do it as quiet as possible. With one of these things up my jacksie I very nearly registered on the Richter scale; quiet was not an option and that's aside from the mandatory swearing and cursing.

To my surprise she agreed and let me use one of the private rooms which meant that I had time and space to convey my feelings about the treatment in privacy. The room also had a TV mounted on the wall of the bedroom and with the toilet door at a certain angle utilising the bathroom mirror I could watch the box whilst doing the doo – luxury. With that all done, I returned to the main ward and called for a pickup off Mum so that I could get a decent night's sleep before the next session of enemas and Papillon.

The next day I was back on the bog again by 9.30 in the morning before being collected by a porter who wheeled me down to the awaiting team of radiographers and Dr Myint. Despite the fact that I was definitely in a far better position than some of the people on the ward and throughout the hospital as a whole, martyrdom was not on my list of new life changes I was going to adhere to.

"Look, Sunny, that really bloody hurt last time. I want some kind of painkiller or muscle relaxant before you go and stick Sputnik back up my arse again!" In the least squeaky voice I could muster – didn't want to look flustered in front of the troops you understand! This request was declined on time and medical backgrounds but after much "Well at least let me have some gas or air for God's sake!" he told one of the nurses to fetch some air should I need it and to wheel it in to the treatment room. The nurse was fine with the whole thing and was there, watching for any indication from me should I need to be aided.

I climbed onto the bed, bent over the hump in the middle and proffered my arse to the world like some sacrificial vase into which a floral tribute to my butt could be rammed. The bum Bongella was applied liberally at my request and the funnel and applicator were inserted with much ooing and arrhing – no air yet. The trolley was wheeled into position, bumping over a couple of wires on the floor. "Jeeessuusss ... watch it!" Still no air! With my bum in place the applicator was removed; the funnel manually straightened to allow the arm of the treatment machine to be lowered into "place" – the best word for it, I think! Then the mandatory exodus by the entire staff – it kind of reminded me of the Monty Python Holy Grail cry to "Run away, run away" when the French are hurling cows at them from the battlements of the castle. If nothing else that thought made me smile, pucker up and take my treatment like a man. With the treatment finished, the faces at the window left their safe haven and returned to the room to retrieve their precious artefact from my bum like Arthur pulling Excalibur from the stone. "Not as bad this time; didn't need the air at all. Sorry about that – being bit of a pussy really!" "Not at all," replied Dr Myint. "You did very well. If you pop back to the ward I'll be with you soon so that we can organise a meeting with Mr Hershman and myself." After a quick thanks to all of the team and a brief discussion with Dr Myint about the best ways to wear my sarong so as to stop it falling down all the time, I returned to the ward and rang the Mum taxi service to come and collect me.

The joint clinic appointment at the Royal Liverpool was arranged for early December 2003. I could hardly believe that over the last six short months my life had changed to the degree that it had. I had discovered quite by accident that I had cancer and not a touch of food poisoning. I had been told that if I did nothing that I would in all likelihood not make the age of thirty-two and my only option was to have my entire colon and my bum hole removed. Then a random chance meeting between Mum and an old friend, who she hadn't seen in ages, who had a friend that just happened to be the only person in the country who could save my arse. Then after six months of drugging and nuking all focusing on this one point. A final meeting with Dr Myint and Mr Hershman at the RLH to discuss whether the months of manic action would bear fruit and that would I qualify for the TEM surgical procedure. Which would hopefully *Save My Arse*! No pressure then?

The day arrived and I was surprisingly ambivalent about the whole thing. The way that my treatment and the entire episode had panned out so far had led me to be even calmer than I had been prior to being ill; stressing was not going to alter the outcome. Mum was excited which was good from my point of view because I could concentrate on her, not the inevitable manual examination that I was going to endure from messrs Myint and Hershman.

I travelled to the hospital with Mum – resistance was futile – and we made our way to the second floor of the impressive Lynda McCartney ward of the LRH. Having checked in we waited in the main reception of the ward before moving to the department seating area. In the second seating area were others who were at various stages of their treatment ranging from initial consultation through to post-operative check-ups. Those who had already had the treatment were by far the calmer of the groups, like battle-hardened soldiers having fought and won their individual campaigns. Eventually, I was called into the examination room, where I was to wait for what seemed an eternity before Dr Myint, Mr Hershman and Margaret sombrely traipsed in like a medical version of Simon, Louis and Sharon from the *X Factor*. It was all laughs and how are yous for the first few minutes – I couldn't resist recalling some of the funnier and more graphic happenings since our last meeting. Then it was time for the up close and personal examination of the target area, "Knees up, on my left side – I know the drill. No arguing though this time please you two. I think my poor arse has gone through enough already – oh, and don't forget, lots of Lube. Ta!"

Dr Myint was the first in there, no by-your-leaves here, just lube and go – I was going to tell him about my new nickname for him – Dr Polo, the mint with the hole – but I felt that he had the advantage at that exact moment in time. Once finished Mr Hershman was next to examine the area where the tumour was originally found. If the treatment had been successful, the area would now be either void of the tumour all together or at least the tumour would be small enough for the TEM surgical procedure to be attempted. The noises emanating from the doctors at least were positive and the examination took less than five minutes in total. With the periscope removed from my bum the doctors retired to their adjoining office to deliberate, leaving me to re-adjust my clothes and pop off to the loo – you never get used to having air blasted up your colon. By the time I had returned, both the doctors had re-entered the examination room – would I get into boot camp or be eliminated here and now? Exciting!

"So, did you come up with your mum again?" asked Mr Hershman.

"Yes, she's sitting outside. Do you want me to go and get her?"

"You can do – it's up to you!" Was the non-committal answer, but I thought what the hell – in for a penny ... Once we had both returned, and the next stage of how are yous and brief catch-ups was dispensed with, I thought that it might be worth getting back to the reason for this cheery gathering. "Anyway, about my arse!" I interrupted.

"Well, from the latest MRI scans and from what we have just seen for ourselves, we can see that the tumour has gone completely. The treatment couldn't have worked any better; the combination stopped its growth and the radiotherapy has cleared the entire area!" said a very happy Mr Hershman.

"The Papillon also destroyed the roots of the cancer without damaging the surrounding tissue," added Dr Myint.

"So are we good to go?" I said, double-checking that there wasn't going to be one of those nasty "but ... " moments. At this point Mr Hershman took on a more serious demeanour and he and Dr Myint exchanged a brief look between one another before he went on. Bugger. I knew it. There is always a but ...

"Whilst we are happy ... more than happy with your progress and the way that your condition has reacted to the treatment," offered Mr Hershman.

"But ... " I added.

"No but ... as such. Whilst we feel that you could qualify for the operation, we have to offer and recommend that you go for the Abdomino Perineal Excision." I heard the breath from Mum, which she must have been holding for ages, escape with an Oh no! I had worked in bars, hotels and for several years door-to-door sales and I knew when someone was, whilst not lying, not telling the whole truth or they didn't believe what they were telling me. He said it a little like when Rachel says yes to a salad when a Chinese takeaway was the other option – what you say and what you mean are often not the same thing. The Abdomino Perineal Excision was the original cutting it all out option, and after all that I had been through to avoid losing my arse, I thought further examination of what my options were was in order.

"Will it work – the TEM?" I asked

"There are no guarantees, but yes!" replied Mr Hershman earnestly

"Are there any guarantees with the big op?"

"Well no. There are never any guarantees whatever we do."

"Do I have a choice?" Just Checking.

"Of course. We will back whatever you decide, but we had to let you know the options so that the final choice would be yours entirely," reiterated Mr Hershman.

"It's not even an option as far as I'm concerned; I haven't gone through all this just to wuss out at the end. I'll take the TEM, if that's all right with you!"

"Thought that you might," said Dr Myint. "Could you just sign this?" From nowhere he produced a clipboard with a sheet of paper citing that I had been given the information and that the decision to go ahead was mine. I didn't even bother with the small print; I was an adult and I was making an informed decision about the quality of life that I hoped I would have once I had beaten the cancer. It is a shame that doctors have to jump through these hoops when they are trying their damnedest to help or save someone's life – this was nothing to do with what was the best option for me; just what the profession at large believed to be the best option for them. Again I found myself feeling extremely lucky that I had found these two doctors and that they were willing to be professionally pilloried in order to help me achieve my goal – and I told them so.

Mum and myself thanked them and we were told that the operation would be in all likelihood towards the end of January 2004, and that we would get a confirmation letter in the next couple of weeks. With some more thank yous and handshakes, we left to go home and crack open some bubbly to celebrate. I spent the trip home on the phone to Rachel, Dad and almost anyone in my mobile address book telling them the good news. Although I had kept my feelings and expectations in check and I knew that I still had a lot to go through before the end; I felt I knew what the champagne was feeling when we popped the cork – and not just in a quick, explosive release of gas way either, for a change!

CHAPTER 26: TOUCHING CLOTH

I had, post-celebration, returned to London to be with Rachel and to get on with getting on. I had to organise myself for the next stage of the treatment and life post-bum op. With all of the excitement about being put forward for the TEM operation early the following year, I had almost forgotten about the little things in life – like Christmas and Christmas shopping – not to mention what to do and where to live after the operation. The Papillon radiotherapy had thankfully done what it said on the tin and had nuked the remainder of the visible tumour and, by the sounds of it, some of the roots of the cancer.

The concern from the doctors' point of view was that this treatment was really designed for polyps and T1surface tumours; my little botty blancmange was bigger and possibly deeper than they had previously dealt with – hence the "throw the book and the kitchen sink at him" approach to the treatment. This seemed to be working well up until this point, although there was a long way to go before my arse was off the endangered list.

Of course, all this treatment had begun to have an effect on my internal workings – I   think this is the most polite way of putting it. I had been nuked every day for five weeks at Bart's and this had caused all the fun with molten larva poos and crispy aromatic arse. My arse and balls still felt as if I had just slid down a sandpaper banister *sans* undies. The chemo was just as much fun with anti-vitamin C attacks, blistering of skin from my lips to my feet, not to mention the little matter of bald balls syndrome. So, I was kind of interested to see what effect the latest couple of sessions of Papillon would have.

The Papillon treatment, whilst in no way as devastating as the conventional treatment, still had its own set of idiosyncrasies. I believe I mentioned the "hands-on approach" was central to the treatment's success as were the actual positioning and dimensions of the apparatus – which in my case was very close to the sphincter muscle. I'm not saying that the treatment had given me a bit of a slack ass but if I dropped my pants and reversed into a shop window I would have stuck to it like an in-car Garfield.

It's the small things that stick in my mind about having cancer – getting or giving spoons in bed for instance. Wind had always been an issue with this cancer from the start; this combined with my treatment meant that my receiving spoons in bed was now a distant and fond memory. I had long since resigned myself to being the giver of the spoons as opposed to the receiver – mainly for health and safety reasons. I was concerned that such was the unpredictability of the fart situation that Rachel, in spoons, ran the risk of potentially losing a limb should I let rip by accident. Now, however, the protective muscle that had been the difference between me being able to function as a quiet, if not occasionally pongy, member of society had been diminished, leaving me with the feeling that I was single-handedly contributing to the depletion of the ozone layer directly above wherever I was.

Auto loos! I bet that you have never given them a second thought; I know I certainly hadn't up until those last couple of weeks! The sort I'm talking of are the ones that have an infrared sensor just on the wall behind you, so that when you get up to leave they flush automatically – cool. Not really! I still would have aches and pains when going to the loo and, I don't know about you, but when I'm in pain on the loo I often rock back and forth like I've been punched in the gut. This is a natural state of affairs apart from when on the auto loo. When I slouched forward in pain from my stomach with my chest nearly flush to the top of my thighs, the loos in my local shopping centre would lose sight of me, and flush automatically! Soggy-bum is not the word but it will suffice for now. Imagine being bideted a couple of times a poo with the water that you are pooing into – not good! What made it worse was that I would jump up causing the loo to flush again often splashing the backs of my legs. Please Mr Toilet Man, change the setting to activate at a greater distance.

Why, I hear you cry, do you continue to use these over enthusiastic loos? One of the other issues with this much treatment and its turning my rear slack was the loss of "pants security". I'll explain. As I had mentioned, the damage to the muscles had been, whilst not dangerous, extensive, and the result had been the deterioration of the muscle control. Uncle Ben told Peter Parker (aka Spiderman) that with great power came great responsibility. Well with great big farts came great concern for the well-being of one's pants. Two words hung over me like a living nightmare – Follow Through. When out and about I would never really be able to tell if I was going to fart or rehash up to a fully fledged number two until it happened. And whilst I would try to clench my cheeks as much as possible, the phrase "oops! that's a wet one!" doesn't cover it. So I had to make sure that I was always close to an establishment which had clean public loos, so that I could make an emergency dash at the drop of a … well, fart if you like. This was often a false alarm, but as an adult would you take the risk, cancer or not, of soiling your underwear? Probably not. So in essence any port in a storm was the way forward. Even if I got the occasional soaking, it was better than a close encounter with a "stool-pool" whilst out shopping or doing whatever it was that I was doing.

You may be wondering why I am mentioning this. The reason is simple – no one had mentioned it to me and I'm pretty sure that there isn't a section on the cancer research website entitled *How to deal with botty gravy*. Like I said, we are all aware that the treatment for cancer is often harsh, but it is the subtle things that most surprised me, and these are the things which those who have the illness must deal with on top of the mandatory side-effects like nausea, hair loss, etc.

I knew that I would have to counter this problem, although gravity cannot be denied or stopped, so I was stuck with reducing the anxiety, and for this I went back to basics – a nappy. Well, that's what I used to call it, but it wasn't really a nappy – more of a panty barrier. Women readers will understand this: white skirt and panties, and you suddenly come on and you have no tampons or pads – not good! Well, imagine that fear ten to twenty times a day for weeks on end. I went for the emergency pad option, which was just several sheets of toilet roll folded and placed strategically within my boxer shorts. I maybe should have gone for some pads and I'm sure there are surgical nappies for adults out there, but to be honest I wasn't overly happy about the situation and didn't want to make it more embarrassing by going into the chemist and ordering some.

I would like to make the point that I never actually fully followed through, although, I have to admit that I was sure that I had definitely been close to touching cloth on several occasions. This, as you could imagine, made Christmas shopping a little nervy – especially down Oxford Street in London.

Being in London was something else that I had to consider, owing to the operation taking place in Liverpool. I had always been confident that I was going to be fine and that me and my arse would rise like the phoenix from the flames of colorectal cancer. I had not, however, planned on what to do once risen. It was only early December, but certain realities needed to be addressed, the most pressing of which being the couch in my flat – was it big enough and comfy enough for me to recover on? I was in no way being flippant about the seriousness of the situation I still found myself in. All fart jokes aside, my cancer was still life-threatening. The tumour was bigger and deeper than first expected, and I was about to undertake a procedure that had in all honesty not been designed for a cancerous tumour the size of mine, especially as we were still not 100% sure as to the extent of the growth of the tumour through the colon wall and whether it had spread into the lymphatic system.

None of this however was within my circle of influence as management consultants and psychologists like to call it. Again, *don't stress about what you can't affect* seemed to be the order of the day, so couch and life post-op were uppermost in my mind. The answer to the couch question was no! My current couch was barely a two-seater and to be completely honest had started to sag in the middle. There was no way I could lay prone and needy on that couch for an hour, let alone a number of weeks. To steal a line from *Jaws*: "We're gonna need a bigger flat!" I told Rachel as much when she got back from work. So, the situation was: three weeks to Christmas, about the same again until the most important operation of my life so far, and we needed to move before the latter to a new and bigger flat. This would not be easy with only one income coming in and no idea as to when I would be able to get another job or if the local council would get off their collective butts and help out with some sort of benefits. Apart from that things were hunky-dory.

As you know, finding somewhere to live is a pain at the best of times. I had already moved during that summer with a chemo bottle attached to my arm and record-breaking temperatures. This time, at least I had no bottle and it was a little cooler, although I was not convinced that the council would get around to granting me any benefits so the flat would have to be cost-effective. However, there were certain aspects of the location and the flat itself that had to be taken into account, not least the size of the couch. I had found a flat not that far from where we were currently living; about £180 per week for a one-bedroom but it did have a nice couch. I had put an offer in and left the estate agent to get on with the details whilst I returned home for the Christmas holidays. I had all but given up shopping for presents in London, as it is just too hectic, both in terms of actually shopping and the need to be close to the loo should I get the call. So I headed home a couple of weeks early to get some shopping in and give Rachel a break from me lounging around using up the bog roll.

CHAPTER 27: CHRISTMAS 2003 – PARTY POPPERS and PAPER PANTS

The schedule for the Christmas period was going to be tight, especially as Rachel was coming to my mum's for the first time this Christmas. I would be back in Chester for just a week, then I would to drive down to Rachel's family on the weekend before Christmas for a couple of parties with all her family, then we would both head back up north for the 23rd. Rachel's mum is based down in Saffron Walden, just outside Stanstead, which is about 200 miles from Chester. Luckily my bum had recovered enough for me to be comfortable sat in a car for several hours at a time otherwise it would have been inflatable doughnut time and I was desperate to avoid them if at all possible. The rubber ring is not a good look anytime of the year, especially at Christmas.

Christmas was going to be a little different this year; we all knew it would be, what with Ben having been away since August, and me with my moody bum. So in traditional Davies manner we went against the common wisdom of a low-key affair and had planned to go all-out. Traditionally we would have dinner at Mum's, with Dad popping round in the morning to do pressies and the rest of the family arriving for Christmas dinner later that day. This year we thought that seeing as Ben was only back for eight or nine days, we would do a mates Christmas as well as the entire north-west clan – it was going to be a classic.

I find Christmas shopping is not an easy thing to do for family and friends because, as you get older, if you want something throughout the year you just go and get it. Everyone knew that I hadn't been working and would have been happy with just a card, especially as this year wasn't about the material things in life at all; it was all about friends and family. This meant that I felt I had to set the example and get something fun for everyone – Rachel's family as well as mine; something that would forever remind them of me whatever the outcome of the operation. Not an easy task! After trawling the novelty Internet sites and deciding that not everyone would like a replica light-sabre – the Jedi type not the oncologist type, I thought that a mooch around the shops in Chester was called for.

Chester is a really nice place to just walk round and shop. You can take in the marvellous mish-mash of architectural styles from over the past 2,000 years. Roman walls surround the city, which has a centre full of Edwardian, Georgian and Victorian buildings converted into shops, bars and restaurants. The shops in the centre are on two levels: the street level topped with original covered walkways which can get a bit low in parts, so if you're over six foot, watch your head. It was on one of these "rows" on Watergate Street that I saw a picture that stopped me in my tracks. It was in a window of a shop I must have walked passed hundreds of times without going in.

The Cartoon Gallery had a small and unassuming exterior but its only window was full of hand-drawn cartoons – not the Disney type but more of the political magazine and paper or amusing birthday card type. The picture that had stopped me and made me laugh out loud in the middle of the row was of mummy and daddy brown bears, lounging under a tree with the baby in deep conversation with a even smaller gold-coloured bear and saying "Winnie the what …?" Obviously in my current situation I thought that this picture just had to be had! I walked in, and was confronted by a mosaic of A4 framed cartoons covering just about every square inch of the walls. I have enough problems buying a card in Clintons but this place was like the biggest and best card shop imaginable, except the cards were actual prints or originals from a number of extremely talented cartoonists. At least half an hour passed without me even noticing, I was just stood looking at all these pictures and giggling to myself. Some of them I recognised from birthday cards, like the Neanderthals playing football at Stonehenge and the stones being the goalposts. Others were original sketches or paintings.

This is it, I thought! I decided that they would be perfect for everyone to hang on the back of their toilet door and have a poo and a grin (not quite have a Coke and a smile but hey). I went to the back of the store where one of the owners/artists was at a sketching board scribbling away at his latest masterpiece. Albert and his wife, Margaret, were co-owners along with a number of other artists from publications such as *Private Eye* and *Punch*. Apart from being two of the nicest people you could ever want to meet, they were more than happy to help me in my quest to make sure that this was going to be a Christmas to remember. Their family, like many others, had been touched by cancer as well, although in a far more serious way than my dodgy arse. Their daughter had a rare and serious form of cancer and was not given much of a chance by anyone – that was several years ago. They had prayed. Now, as I've said, I'm not a religious person, but the fact still remained that they had their faith and they *still* had their daughter who was now fine. We talked for ages and had a right giggle picking out ten framed cartoon sketches for my family and friends. Margaret wrapped all of them, *with bows*, and they helped me carry them out to the taxi that I had to call to transport them all home. I was over the moon with the presents and couldn't wait to see people's faces when they got their individual pictures.

I also got the chance to go out for a couple of nights on the town in Liverpool with Rob, before going back down south. Rob is the cool, good-looking one of the mates that my brother, Ben, and I share. I remember when I was back from Uni and the lads would head out on the town, I was always the one at the back, the fat friend (although I wasn't that fat at the time). Now that we were older things hadn't really changed. This did mean, however, that he would go to, and get invited to, the better parties and bars. We visited the trendy bars in Liverpool and the thing that I remember most was feeling old. One night we went to a pre-Christmas fashion show at one of the "cool" bars in Liverpool – invite only job! Once in we mingled – well he mingled; I sort of hung round and tried to look interesting. I was introduced to his girlfriend at the time and her mates, all young and beautiful and we generally had a giggle. It was the sort of bar which had soap stars and footballers hanging around – apparently Girls Aloud were there but I wouldn't have known them at the time, if they were stood in front of me.

The thing that stands out in my memory of that night was the toilet. I was still at the mercy of my bowels and the slackness of my arse muscles was still an issue. I had, by this time, essentially turned into a girl – I had to sit to piss (just to be on the safe side you understand). I would go to the little boys room and into a cubicle and be confronted by a disaster zone. This is a common problem throughout the majority of public places nationwide – blokes piss on the toilet seats. The ladies might find it hard to believe that the seat was down at all, but your average lager drinking male is not that bright. Whilst there are the standing options, for some reason some men feel that they are not up to the public showing of tackle and hide in the cubicle to pee – fair enough. What annoys me is that they seem to be incapable of lifting the seat to piss therefore covering it in urine.

Normally, this is, at worst, an inconvenience – just a case of having to grab a fistful of paper and wipe everything down, place a couple of sheets over the seat and sit. The two things you need to perform this operation are paper and time. Surprisingly I had paper, but time was not something that I could rely on. When the call came I wouldn't know whether it would be for a number one or two; whichever it would finally be I would have to sit, and there was always a sense of urgency attached to the call, especially when out in public. It was a nightmare! I spent a lot of the night in the toilet, not because I needed to go but because I would have to pre-empt the urge and spend five minutes wiping down the cubical before actually going – often to no avail.

I understand and accept that if you live with a female, she will make your life hell if the toilet seat is left up, although I don't recall a bloke complaining about the seat being down. But lads, come on please, when in public, try to remember to lift the seat before you wee. God forbid, should you ever get this illness, trust me, emergency wipe downs are not a welcome addition to the things that you will have to deal with, especially when in a rush. Remember the toilet seat code – Stand **Up**, Sit **Down.**

The first stop on this multi-venue Christmas was Rachel's mum's house in Saffron Walden, before heading to her gran's (known as Ga Ga – no radio) house where Rachel's uncle Jon was coming over with his wife Julie and their three boys Jamie, Miles and Guy. I always thought it was funny how it had worked out that Rachel's mum had three girls and her brother, uncle John, had three boys – spooky. This obviously made for a full house at Ga Ga's and the entire day was a cracker (no Christmas pun intended). We had the PlayStation dance mat out, which was a laugh after lots of booze and food. It was the first time that I had been with Rachel's family for a Christmas party, and it was a great day all round. I played with the lads, especially Miles and Guy. They were a little younger than the rest, who had these cool foam-saucer guns. Presents were exchanged and all in all it was a perfect start to the Christmas period

– next stop was for Rachel and I to head back home to see Ben and get our mates round for stage two of the Christmas tour.

Ben had flown in from Jakarta on the morning of the 23rd and so was there when I arrived, which was great. We chatted about his teaching and life out in Indonesia, as well as discussing my progress and the next stage of the treatment, before he succumbed to the thirteen hour flight and crashed for the night. I popped into town with Ben on Christmas Eve so that he could change some money and get some final pressies. We went into a travel agency to get his last three months' worth of savings changed into sterling. He had literally an inch of notes to be exchanged, something like three million rupiah – he got £27 in total. His little face dropped as he walked away with two notes and some change. "I'll get the beers in then!" I said, trying to suppress my laughter.

The plan for Christmas Day was that our friends Jay and Rob would come over Christmas morning, as would Dad with Jean and Nana. Hayley, my stepsister, was also coming over, as was Janet and Ian from across the road after that. This would happen late morning after we did pressies – in theory! This best-laid plan, even without the aid of any mice, soon went the way of the Dodo, as people started to show up in waves. Dad et al. did arrive first and once I had gotten Nana's G&T (my job being the eldest grandchild) we cracked on with the opening of pressies, champagne was retrieved from the fridge and the smoked salmon thingies that Rachel, Ben and I had made earlier that morning were consumed en masse. Mum still has our Christmas sacks from when we were young and I still get excited about being presented with this big bag of things to unwrap every year, even though now there are more socks and less Lego.

I started on mine as did Ben and everyone else, then the doorbell rang and the lads arrived. They had just started on their pressies when Hayley turned up, then came Janet and Ian with a couple of their grown-up sons – it was sheer pandemonium in the best way possible. People coming in were confronted with bodies, pressies and paper strewn all over the lounge floor, champagne popping, people laughing, hugs and kisses being freely given and received gratefully – it truly was a fantastic way to start Christmas Day. Everyone loved the pictures, which was handy, and got on with getting as much Christmas spirit down themselves as possible. The thing that I thought was great was the way that nearly everyone had gotten me a card with some reference to arses, poos, farts, etc.

No one shied away and everyone took on the philosophy that we were dealing with this in the only way that we knew how – by having a bit a laugh at the situation and being as positive and upbeat as we could. It worked out that way, and I nearly had a quibbly bottom lip moment on a number of occasions, I was that happy. Ben bought us all traditional Indonesian prayer shirts, which we immediately put on, and he also got me a pack of disposable paper pants. These I had to put on straight away, but over my trousers à la Superman – very fetching. Once the madness had abated somewhat, I made a little time to speak to everyone individually before the party broke up. Dad went back to have dinner at his, and Janet and Ian went back across the road to have their family meal, leaving just the boys, Rachel and Hayley for lunch at ours. Something happens to the stomach on Christmas Day that allows it to swell to the size of a two-man tent. You eat more than you would normally have in a week. Crackers were cracked, hats were donned, the crap jokes inside were told and more booze was downed – what more is there? Once we had consumed enough food to feed a small country, we retired to the lounge to recuperate and sneak in a post-dinner snooze before heading to the local pub for a quick Christmas-night pint.

Boxing Day wasn't going to be any quieter than Christmas Day because the Liverpool lot, Uncle Billy, Aunty Anne, Granddad and the rest of them, were over to continue the party. Aside from the cold turkey, there were hams, pies, salads, sandwiches and more wine. Bearing in mind that I was about to have a large hole cut out of my colon I figured that I might as well take advantage of being able to eat what I liked whilst I still could. I didn't know what effect the operation would have on my short-term ability to eat and go to the loo, so it was very much the case of "when in Rome".

Ben flew back to Jakarta on the 29th of December, leaving Rachel and I to spend New Year in Liverpool. That wasn't the end to our Christmas family tour however. Rachel's Dad lives with his partner, Chris, over in Norfolk and was having a party for his daughters and their boyfriends to do a late Christmas and celebrate his birthday, on the first weekend in January. So from the Northwest we set off to Norfolk to meet up with Rachel's sister Ruth and her boyfriend James (Gill to us) and her youngest sister Faye. Once again it was a great weekend with an obscene amount of fantastic home-cooked food and quality wines.

Once that was over we had to scoot back to London; we eventually got back to our flat on the 6th of January. I had received a call from the estate agent during that week saying that the flat had fallen through. Back at our flat in London I had also gotten confirmation of my dates for the operation. I was to report to the Royal Liverpool on the 28th of January, with the operation to take place on the 30th. Obviously I was happy to get the dates confirmed; the only problem was that we had to be moved out by the 24th just a couple days earlier, and we still didn't have anywhere to move to. On the plus side, this meant that I was far too busy and stressed with trying to find somewhere to live to worry about the little matter of my arse. I eventually found a nice little flat in Canada Water; again it was just up the road from where we already were in south-east London, but it was next to a canal, which meant that it would at least be quiet. The couch wasn't huge, but by this time I was past caring and just needed to get in somewhere nice; even if the flat cost a little more than we wanted it was worth it owing to its close proximity to a shopping centre and the tube.

I left Rachel and our new flat on Monday 26th to head back to Mum's in Chester to prepare for the culmination of months of treatment and anxiety. By the end of this week I would know whether all of the radiotherapy, chemotherapy, burnt skin, blistered hands and feet, illness, pain and distress to my family and friends had been worth it

CHAPTER 28: CRUNCH TIME!

The big day had finally arrived and I was dropped off at the hospital mid morning on Wednesday the 28th. Mum returned home with the promise to pop back later that day and I made my way inside and reported to the reception. My schedule for the next couple of days was to spend time on limited, and then no, food as my colon was emptied. On Friday the 30th I would be operated on and hopefully be out within a week maximum. Dr Myint and Mr Hershman were confident of a successful outcome to the operation, and I was confident in them – so all in all I was not in the least concerned about the whole procedure.

After an hour or so of waiting around in various reception rooms, with adequate reading material that I had brought with me to hand – different hospital, same wait – I was called in to start the signing in process. I was a little concerned that they had managed to lose my details between reception and the signing in room, approximately 12 feet away, but I didn't dwell as I had other things on my mind. Once the paperwork was complete I was led into a side room to have my blood taken. There were three of them in the room – a male and two young female nurses. The male nurse was a senior student and was helping train the two young girls in blood taking etc. I was asked whether I minded if the girls could take the blood, as they needed real practise as well as just having to observe. I agreed. They were both young and attractive girls, if not a tad on the orange side owing to some overzealously applied fake tan – not an uncommon state of affairs in Liverpool.

I had by this time given blood to so many doctors and nurses all over the country I couldn't see it being a problem, and to be honest blood taking was a lot nicer than some of the things trainees had done to me over the previous six months. The first attempt didn't go too well; neither did the second, third or fourth. So the other girl tried and failed several times. By this time the inside of my elbow was beginning to bruise and swell with all of the failed attempts to find a vein. I think they were just nervous about it hurting me and therefore weren't just going straight in. The senior student nurse apologised and took over but he was worse, in that although eventually blood was taken he did not care if it hurt and came at it like Norman Bates's dagger action in the shower scene. That little escapade took nearly half an hour and had left the inside of my right arm looking like I was heroin junkie extra from *Trainspotting*.

At around 4 pm that afternoon I was eventually taken up to the ward and shown where I was to be housed for the next couple of days. The RLH is older than the cancer ward that I was in at the Clatterbridge centre and the design of the wards reflected this. My ward was eight floors up and separated into rooms that held six. I was shown to my bed and nodded my hellos to the other gents there. I was briefed on how my diet would be reduced to nil by mouth by the following afternoon, to the extent that when they brought round some little jelly pots I had to have one without any fruity bits in.

The population of the ward was again older than me and I started chatting to the guys about what they were in for – very jailbird-like. I briefly chatted to a guy in his late fifties or early sixties who had just had the *big operation* for colon cancer at the start of the week. He looked rough and he admitted that he didn't feel any better than he looked. He was bandaged, wired up and as pale as a ghost. I passed over the details of what was happening to me as he might have been a bit annoyed, plus I'm not a doctor so couldn't comment on his condition. (As I have mentioned, the procedure that I was going to have is not a guarantee or an option in some cases.) I was only in that room for about half an hour when they decided that I was in the wrong room and moved me. The next room was pretty much the same; again, a six-bedded affair, although a couple of the lads in there were a little younger – mid forties/early fifties. They were in for a number of reasons; the old guy next to me had tubes emanating from his stomach into a bell-jar-type apparatus. This was filling up with a nasty-looking dark green (mint-sauce- type green) almost black liquid from a colon infection caused by a botched operation to remove cancer a couple of years earlier. Though, a couple of the younger gents were in for lesser ailments such as piles and one guy for his varicose veins. The bed had the mandatory paper-looking sheets, a small side cupboard and a little TV on an extendable arm above the bed, which had Sky movies, as well as some terrestrial channels for which credit could be bought.

A staff nurse came through and went through the various check-in protocols and questions such as what medicine I was on etc. I was handed some surgical stockings to wear to ensure against blood clots, like long flight socks for DVT. I tried them on and took them off after two minutes as they were definitely too small and were doing the opposite to what they were supposed to do by actually cutting off all circulation. I opted for my more usual attire of sarong and T-shirt and left it at that. That night I was refused a sleeping tablet owing to it not being on my chart and so watched movies and listened to old Frank's bell jar bubbling away next to me until five in the morning.

I know I have said this before but if your doctor generally says, "all you need is some rest and recuperation" then why do the nurses insist on waking everyone up at like 6.30 in the morning? At that time in the morning, after an hour of sleep I don't want to be woken up, have a cup of weak tea or get up so they can change my sheets. This is not restful or helpful to anyone's well-being especially if you're ill and need to bloody sleep.

Thursday the 29th was a case of sitting around, not eating and being visited by Mum, Dad, et al., and reading. Mr Hershman came to see me, which made me feel better, as he was excited about trying out his new scalpel on me and explained about how it wasn't a knife at all but used ultrasonic sound waves to almost dissolve the tissue thus helping to reduce scarring. I had a small tap cannula inserted, poorly, into the back of my hand for taking blood etc. (arm was of no use now because they couldn't see any veins through the bruising) which was already beginning to hurt my hand. I had utmost confidence in my surgical team but I have to admit the rest of the show so far was all a bit like amateur hour, and to make it worse the nurses didn't seem to care.

Mr Hershman went through my schedule for the next day: the anaesthetist was coming to see me at 5.30 am; I was to be taken down at around 8 am with the operation booked in for 8.45 am. If all went well I should be back in the ward for between 1 and 2 pm that afternoon. At least with the anaesthetic I will get a couple of hours' kip, I thought.

That night I was allowed a sleeping pill: I'd had a word with Dr Myint when he popped in to see me. Even with the pill I must have only managed to get two hours in before I was woken at 5.30 am by the anaesthetist. They wheeled me down at just before 8 am to the pre-op room and by this time I had changed into a backless surgical gown and been given new longer surgical stockings. There were at least four members of the surgical team in the operating room including the anaesthetist, but no Mr Hershman yet. I was rolled off the wheeled trolley onto the operating table and told to just chill for a couple of minutes whilst we waited for Mr Hershman. Aside from what can only be described as stirrups similar to those used when giving birth, which I eyed rather nervously, I noticed the way that the team were very calm and organised and some of this transferred itself to me. I would be a liar if I said that now I'd actually found myself on the slab, I wasn't a tad nervous. One of the team turned to me, seeing me anxiously eyeing the stirrups, and said that Mr Hershman was simply the best surgeon that they had worked with and that with him at the helm I was going to be fine. He arrived and we had a quick chat and giggle before we commenced. I made him promise that he wouldn't remove my arse unless it was a matter of life or death, which he did. He told me that Sunny was coming over from Clatterbridge especially to see me and hopefully might catch a bit of the operation, and then came the anaesthetic. I only managed to get to about five on the countdown from ten before I was gone.

CHAPTER 29: IT WAS NO PIPE DREAM

I have been under a general anaesthetic on a couple of occasions for minor things like sinus operations and I always remember the feeling of coming round being different from simply waking up in the morning. Waking up from a general anaesthetic, I think, must be like being born to full consciousness – one moment oblivion, the next you're awake.

Lying there on a trolley in the recovery room I tried to centre myself and calm my mind. "OK," I thought. "I'd better check that everything is still where it should be!" Similar to the walking out the door pre-holiday – ticket, passport, money – checklist but concentrated more on my arse than what's in my back pocket. First off I ran my hand tentatively down my stomach to see if there were any large bandages or bags attached. No! Phew! I then lifted myself slightly onto my shoulder blades and heels and slipped my hand under my gown just to confirm that I had indeed still got a bum. I carefully let me backside return to the bed with a satisfied and grateful sigh of relief. Mr Hershman and Dr Myint had done it. They had managed to save my arse. At that stage I had no thoughts about remission, the cancer coming back or other things that may or may not go wrong; I was just over the moon to be still in possession of my arse; my rusty sheriff's badge, my chocolate starfish; my poop shoot was safe and I was a very happy chappy.

The thing about consciousness is that once you are, conscious that is, you start to be aware of things that were done to you when you weren't, and once again the little voice in my head was saying all was not well. I took a breath and looked down to see if my initial examination had missed anything important. I couldn't see anything that was obvious from under the covers at first – just a yellow pipe that was protruding from under the sheet and leading off the bed. *This yellow pipe*, my consciousness continued, *must lead to somewhere*! That was when I decided that I had better discover its source. The pipe did indeed run under the top sheet, which I pulled back, and I followed it under my leg and then up between my legs. It was at that point my dick woke up and to our joint horror the pipe was coming from out of it. I had a large pipe, width of a normal straw that you would find in McDonald's for example, emanating from the business end of my willy, and it chaffed somewhat! I threw off the bed cover and gently touched the end of my old boy, in the same consoling way that you might consol a pet on the operating table of a vet. It will be all right little fella, I could hear myself thinking. I looked up from my violated penis and called over one of the male nurses who was making his way over to me, having noticed that I had woken up.

"Excuse me!" Willy pipe or not, manners are important I thought. I am English after all. "Excuse me – there is a long yellow pipe sticking out of my Jap's eye," I squeaked.

"Yes that's a catheter. It's to help you pass fluids until you are recovered," he said.

"I don't care what it is or what it does; no one said that they were going to stick a pipe down my old boy's throat – I would have remembered! Can you take it out; I didn't sign up for no willy pipe malarkey."

"It's there for you own good. Your bladder is in need of help until both it and your bowel stabilise a bit. You really shouldn't feel much discomfort at all once it's in," he said appeasingly. I was not happy and told him as much, but at least it was a short-term bag protruding from the end of my old boy and not a permanent bag instead of an arse. So all in all, I couldn't complain.

I was back, bag an' all, on the ward by 1.45 pm, nearly six hours after being taken down. The operation itself lasted just over four hours and had looked to be a success at this stage from my point of view. I had even started to get the hang of the catheter, or "Piss Pouch" as I had now christened it. You know the feeling of abandonment you get, as an adult, when you go for a wee in the sea? That warm feeling, the feeling of freedom, a regression back to when you could go to the loo whenever because you were a small child; it was a little like that except with the discomfort of a bloody big pipe up ya dick. It seemed that I just kept having little wees. I got to the stage were I would have a swig of water and time how quickly it would be turned yellow and expelled down the pipe into a bag about the size of a hot water bottle attached to the end.

Mum showed at just gone 2 pm and I rang Rachel as soon as I was able, to let her know that I was OK and that the Sunday papers were safe for the foreseeable future – she was understandably quite emotional and was looking forward to seeing me the next day. Dad and the rest of the family were going to be popping in and out over the weekend but for that day it was only Mum, purely because no one was sure how tired I'd be etc. Mum asked if I was in any pain and at that point I wasn't really; my bum felt like I'd shat a bowling ball but apart from that I was OK; I think the anaesthetic was still in my system and once mum left I went to sleep, for a short while.

I woke in time for dinner, around 5.30 pm, which I declined on account that the last thing I wanted to do was encourage my bowel to test my new bum out, just yet. The pain I was experiencing wasn't the post-operation cutting, scarred sort of pain; it was more muscular in nature. Yes, I was sore around my bum and internally, but it was my chest and back that were the surprise centres of pain from my point of view. It made me wonder what sort of positions I had been in during the four hour operation. On top of the muscle pain, I was losing sensation in my legs owing to the bloody stockings cutting off my circulation, which I was not allowed to take off as they were supposed to be helping, and the catheter in the back of my hand was still giving me gyp.

As for the Piss Pouch, don't get me started – it was really beginning to get up my, well, willy. Yes the constant weeing into a bag was still amusing but I was having a bit of leakage around where it entered my shaft. On top of that, any time I needed to roll over or get out of bed it would have to be moved or come walkies with me. On the plus side, the sarong was a winner for going roaming with the bag as the pipe just stuck out of the gap were it was folded over – handy!

What with the soreness, the coughing and spluttering of my fellow patients, the bubbling of my neighbour's gut and having to be aware that rolling over could be bad with the pipe where it was, sleeping was a bit of a nightmare as you could imagine on that Friday night, even with painkillers and sleeping tablets. I probably managed a couple of hours before waking up just before 6 am on the Saturday morning. The tea lady came round and then I was encouraged to get up and shower whilst the sheets were changed before the breakfast trolley came round at 7.30. I'm not the biggest sleeper in the world but I was definitely getting a bit grumpy by this stage. Not including the operation I had probably only had eight to ten hours' sleep since coming in on the Thursday, three days earlier. I hadn't eaten since Thursday night and having to get up and be talked to like a five-year-old was not adding to my current disposition. In the shower there were dirty paper towels on the floor, as well as used soap and shampoo wrappers. It was not too dissimilar to a shower that I'd shared with six others, in a company house a few years earlier. I'd brought flip-flops with me just in case and kept them on whilst showering, which is a bit tricky with a yard of tubing and a half full (or was it half empty?) piss pouch attached to the end of your knob, I can tell ya.

Once showered, I returned to the bed, which hadn't been changed yet, and so waited on a chair that was next to the bed whilst it was being finished. I declined breakfast again because I just wasn't hungry and on top of that my hand was hurting again from the badly inserted hand catheter and I was still not convinced that the Piss Pouch was attached correctly as it was still pretty uncomfortable and I was not happy with the seepage. I asked the nurse in charge whether I could get the catheters removed and got turned down again.

"Have you been to the toilet yet?" she asked.

"Yes, all the time," I said gesturing to the half full Piss Pouch.

"Have your bowels moved yet? I know your bladder works but we have to wait until your bowels are working again before removing the catheter."

"I haven't eaten in three days and just had big hole cut out of my colon – of course I haven't been yet. I've got nothing to go with." I pointed out in as calm a manner as I could.

"Once you've been we'll take it out, and as for the hand catheter we might still need to take blood so it should stay where it is!" With that she turned on her heal and marched off in a "how dare he question me" type manner.

Just before lunch a couple of the nurses rushed in, plumped pillows, moved bed tables and generally busied themselves before the consultants swanned in with their gaggle of junior doctors – it was a right *Carry On*! It reminded me of the pomp and ceremony surrounding the royal handshaking at the end of Wimbledon, when the ball-boys and girls are presented to the royal patrons. Luckily, my lot – Hershman and Myint – weren't due to pop round till later that day, and to be honest I'm not sure if Sunny would know pomp if it came up and said "Hi. I'm pomp." I tried to catch an hour's sleep before the visitors arrived.

Rachel and Mum came up, as did my dad, even Granddad came up with Uncle Billy and Aunty Anne. I'd given family and friends wide notice: don't send flowers, bring wine gums. So by early evening I was waist deep in Maynard's and Bassett's – these I felt I could eat. During the day I had accidentally whacked my hand catheter on something – probably going to the loo in a vain attempt to "move my bowels". It was now really sore, had started to bleed internally and had filled with blood. They still wouldn't take it out. I had a little dinner, but the first poo of this new era was nowhere in sight, and I was pretty annoyed with the pain by the time the shift change happened around seven that evening.

The two nurses that came on shift were the same two from the night before, and I had got on with really well with them. I'd had enough of both of the catheters by this point and decided to act. I called one of them over and decided to try the sympathy vote. It didn't work. So I went for plan B:

"I'm over eighteen and therefore as an adult I'm able to make the decision as to whether I accept or decline treatment – correct?" I ventured. The nurse eyed me wearily. "Well, as an adult I'm telling you to take out both the tap in the back of my hand and my dick pipe, because I'm sure both were put in wrong and are hurting like a bugger." She was not happy, and I was nearly going to throw the "I'll sue you" line at them, which I really didn't want to do because at every turn throughout my illness all the staff of all of the hospitals had been a credit to their profession. This however was, for want of a better phrase, taking the piss and it was going to end here and now.

First, out came the hand tap, which spurted blood about a metre across the bed, and then came the Piss Pouch. "This has a small balloon which is expanded internally to keep it secure and safe," she informed me. "So it was a good job that you didn't try to remove it yourself because it wouldn't ha … Oh! That came out without me even trying. That's strange; it mustn't have been inserted properly – sorry about that!" No shit, I thought as I glared at her. I had been through a lot since being ill and I was annoyed that no one was prepared to take me at my word when I said I was in pain. With the tube out I got up and went for a piss the traditional way – standing!

The Sunday was much the same as every other day as far as I could tell. Woken up at stupid o'clock, told to get out of bed and shower, before having dodgy coffee and some breakfast. I had my fair share of visitors again that day. Rachel came over again before heading back to London and work, as did Mum and Geoff. I'd decided that I was not going to sit around in bed all day, so I took myself off for a wander. There were a couple of shops and a café with chairs above the reception area of the hospital. Now that I was pipe free, I felt a little more comfortable about being seen by Joe Public. I decided to take the stairs down from the eighth floor so that I could stretch my legs a little. I was happy with the overall pain level in my back and lower bits, though a walk would probably be one of those things that I would have been advised against by the staff. So I didn't ask. It was nice to sit and read the paper whilst having a good cup of coffee. I'd missed most of the weekend's football results owing to being operated on and stuff, and I needed to know how Liverpool were faring since the start of the new year – once again we were running close but I was afraid that come May there would be no cigar. That done, I got the lift back up to the ward with the decision made that I was simply not going to get better being in this hospital and that tomorrow I would be out of here, with or without their approval.

Monday morning came and I refused to get out of bed so that they could change my sheets. I had only been in them twenty-four hours and they were warm and comfy and I was so tired that I was just going to go back to sleep. "But they are dirty," said the cleaner.

"See that blood on the floor by my bed?" I said, pointing at the small dried patch. "That has been on the floor since Saturday – clean that if you want something to do and leave me alone!" I'm not great without sleep.

"Not my job!" huffed the cleaner as she stomped off. What about the toilets and showers, I thought darkly, rolling over onto my side and pulling the sheets up to my neck – not your job either?

My sleep had only lasted an hour or so before Mr Hershman came to see me. We talked about the success of the operation in more detail. I bitched about the catheters and the way that some of the evening staff treated the older patients as a nuisance when they were in pain. Essentially I was not happy and I told him that I wanted out – today! He said that I could leave around two o'clock that afternoon if the blood tests and other bits and bobs came back OK. This is one of the advantages of the operation that I had. The poor sod I had met on my first day, who looked like he'd been hit by a bus after the traditional operation they'd recommended to me, had been in a week and would be in hospital for a while longer. I'd been chopped on Friday and would escape on Monday – bargain. (Once again, do realise that I am a stubborn pain in the arse and that both the time in hospital and the choice of operation were mine alone and not recommended by the greater medical community.)

Two o'clock came and Mum arrived to take me home. I'd asked her to bring a pillow for me to sit on in the car as my bum and lower back were a little more sore than they had been on the Sunday, not that I mentioned this to the doctors. I requested some hospital strength pads for the bum leakage I was experiencing (no proper toilet action yet, but I did have a strange sort of goo emanating from my bum that looked sort of like marmalade) and a medical ring to sit on. These were turned down and after two hours waiting for the drugs that I was told the pharmacy had ready for me, I got some fibre gel and some codeine. That was it. No *by the way do this or try that*; just a two hour wait for some standard-strength painkillers and something to make my poo squidgy, both of which I could get over the counter.

That was it. I lost my rag and screamed blue murder at the pharmacist. Yes I was in some pain, mainly around what felt like my lower back. Yes, I'd had very little sleep in nearly a week. The thing that really got me annoyed, aside from the sheer incompetence of the whole show, was that no one seemed to care what I did next. If you buy some aspirin in a pharmacist, you get a whole booklet of instructions, written in several languages, on what to do. I'd just had a major cancer operation that was at best a bit of a risk; I was still in some pain, which was fine but obvious after having an inch and a bit being removed from my colon; and the best that the hospital could do for me was a crappy painkiller (not the good stuff) and some poo softener – I'd still not been! What was going on in their tiny minds? What sort of precautions should I be taking against infection? What sort of diet would be best for someone with a large hole in their arse? When should I be worried if no poo came? What possible side-effects are there that I should be looking out for? I admit that for large parts of this journey I had not done the most reading around the subject, but there wasn't as much as a pamphlet on where to buy good bog roll – nothing! I was not a happy bunny and I let them know it.

I'm not sure that this lack of post-operational information is common or not but it seems to me that if more information were given to people, they would have less need to be in hospital or ring their doctors about stuff that might be obvious. I mean, not even being given some dietary information after a colon operation seemed negligent to say least. You have to bear in mind that I hadn't really eaten or slept for three or four days so I was not in the most consolatory of moods.

With my "hairdryer" bit done and dusted, I eased myself carefully into Mum's car. She'd brought the MG so the cushion was welcome. We went home.

CHAPTER 30: TWO STEPS FORWARD, ONE STEP BACK

Being back at home after the operation was a little strange. I had been fighting against the threat of having my life changed forever, my arse being removed or possibly the cancer spreading and finishing the job properly, for months, and now I was on my mum's couch with a cuppa. The emotional stress and the anticipation of the preceding months seemed far more intense than the high gained from achieving the positive result that we were fighting for. It was far more a feeling of *thank God that's over* than *dancing on the ceiling* happiness. Having done nothing but go straight to bed on the Monday afternoon, come Tuesday I thought that I should get on with things and test myself and go for a little wander. My bits felt OK – sore, admittedly, with some residual muscle pain down my back, but not bad all things considered. So I walked down to the local shop to grab some fresh air and the paper. By the time I got back I noticed that the pain in my back had increased a bit but to be honest that didn't seem unreasonable owing to the battering that it had taken over the weekend.

By the end of the week I still had not been for a number two and the pain in the base of my back had increased to the stage that sitting up was actually hurting. Although I had not managed to do the do in toilet terms I had still been visiting the throne eight to ten times a day, all to no avail, which with an increasingly sore back was beginning to piss me off a bit. The saying "no pain, no gain" is fine apart from when it's pain and no gain! I started to try and keep myself amused when sitting on the loo waiting for nothing to happen – mobile phone games, texting mates, resting my chin on my fist in a "to poo or not to poo – that is the question" type position; still no movement.

It was 2 am on Saturday the 7th of January, just over a week after my operation when the first poo sighting was officially recorded. The pain was pretty intense and it took ages, and all just for a peanut's worth. And then just like buses three came round the U-bend all together. I was back on the toilet at 3 am, 4 am and at about 5.30 am. All with a lot of pain for little reward; the last visit felt like I was giving birth to quads and I mean the bikes not the kids. By Sunday I was incapacitated on the couch; I'd not slept properly since the night of the peanuts and the pain in the base of my back had increased considerably. My only positive was that a Macmillan nurse was coming to visit me the next day.

The Macmillan nurses are experts in cancer. They are trained to help people with cancer and support their families. Part of the Macmillan nurse's job is to meet with people as soon as possible after a cancer diagnosis, or in my case after the operation itself, and offer help and support for as long as it is needed. Some of the things that they look at are ways to control pain and other symptoms, give advice about cancer treatments and how to cope with side-effects, provide emotional support and offer practical help, including advice on benefits and other financial matters. My nurse was called Jackie and she was brilliant.

Whilst I talk a lot, I often do so just to keep from being bored, not to inform. With Jackie she asked the right questions and listened to the answers without judging. She didn't think that I was exaggerating about the level of pain that I was in and took me at my word. She immediately got onto the district nurse and onto my surgical team's registrar, who suggested an anti-inflammatory drug used by arthritis sufferers. The thinking was that it was referred pain from the operation and with the anti-inflammatory drugs things would settle down. I wasn't convinced about the referred pain theory, as I felt the pain in the base of my back, but for now all painkillers were welcome. Just to be on the safe side we got some morphine tablets and some ora-morph (bottles of morphine that I was to use for breakthrough pain). We talked about the little things like the fact that I had not really been properly for a poo yet, and when I tried I couldn't go for a number one and number two in the same sitting.

Once she had left with a promise to come back in a couple of days, I cracked open the morphine and went for a snooze. The next day I experimented a little with the dosage and timings of the tablets. I didn't want to drink any of the ora-morph as I wanted to keep it for when I was really sore, but I did manage a proper "movement" later on the Tuesday afternoon, eleven days after the operation. The pain in my back was steady on the Wednesday but felt different from before. It was more acute in sensation than general and the sitting on the loo just put more pressure on my spine which in turn caused more pain. Aside from this, the painkillers were beginning to bung me up which meant that the visits, still eight to ten a day with varying degrees of success, were taking longer and hurting more and more. I had the anti-inflammatory drugs and antibiotics to look after the operational scarring but the sitting down was really beginning to hurt – this I passed on to Jackie.

I woke up at 5.40 am on the Thursday and went straight to the loo. The ora-morph bottle was now on the cistern so that when I was most in pain, when I was sat down, I could have a swig. I tried to go back to sleep and succeeded for a couple of hours but when I awoke I had a dead butt cheek and left leg. I found myself once again in the "don't want to eat because that will make me go to the loo" situation and so missed brekky. This was not wise as the antibiotics, that I was on, required them to be taken with food, and so I promptly threw up as per instructions on the box. Not good! So come lunchtime I was famished and this helped keep the next set of pills down. At around mid afternoon the hospital rang and told me that, owing to the information being given to them by Jackie, I was to be re-admitted – straight away. By five that afternoon I was back in my old bed, next to Bell Jar guy – who was feeling a lot better thank you very much – and in time to catch Mr Hershman. He explained that he was looking at opening the sucher the next day to relieve any excess pressure built up that might be causing the referred pain in my back. We talked about my inability to multitask on the toilet – pass water and poo before passing out with pain. He said that it looked like the cancer had gone. This was obviously great news, although, in the drugged up, off my face on morphine and in great pain state of mind and body, I didn't do the cartwheels I think he was expecting.

I was concerned rather than happy, I know that sounds ungrateful and it probably was, but I needed to know what was wrong with my back. He said that on very rare occasions the digging around that close to the spine might disturb some cartlilage or tissue in the lower spinal region. I thought someone should have mentioned that little pearl a little earlier. Had this possibility been presented to me prior to the operation, there was a very good chance that I would not have been back in hospital at all. I'd been walking around all over the place, thinking that exercise would be a good thing, sitting on the loo (well straining like a professional gurner), essentially not overly looking after my back in the same way I might have, had I known that there were potential spinal consequences. In fact the pain would have been mentally less stressful and self-explanatory had we known. I wasn't happy at the pain and being back in hospital, especially one that I didn't trust when I was sober, let alone in the mental vegetable state I was currently in. None of it eased my sense of foreboding. I was to go down to be operated on in the morning and this meant that I was not to eat, which was fine apart from the fact that I couldn't take my antib's and anti-inflammatories, thereby removing any chance that I might have had of grabbing a couple of hours' kip that night. The fact that having the pills without food would have made me violently ill didn't stop the staff giving me them anyway. I had to refuse to take them because the nurses obviously hadn't read what was on the label – very reassuring!

It was a bit of a mad twenty-four hours all in all. I watched *Night of the Living Dead* on Sky that evening whilst listening to the bubbling stomach bell jar – not a prophecy I hoped. I went gingerly to the loo at two, four, and six before going for a shower at seven and then down to the operating theatre at 8.30 am. The date was Friday 13 February. You can see why I was concerned. I awoke from the anaesthetic and was back in the ward by eleven this time, with my bum still where it should be. Which was nice.

At around midday the staff came round with pills and then some soup for lunch. Although I was hungry I hadn't seen Mr Hershman yet and didn't know whether eating was the best thing for me at that time, although the staff assured me that I was OK to eat. The problem by that stage was that I had lost all confidence in the staff at the hospital; I don't know if this was because of the paranoia which accompanies hugh amounts of drugs or just their track record where I was concerned. Either way, I delined the antibiotics owing to the no food and chucking up situation, although they again tried to make me take them anyway. "I've just had another colon operation. Surely you must know that the pills will make me wretch and possibly do some internal damage!" I said to one of the dispensing nurses. She just grunted and when I asked for some of my painkillers (only the prescribed morphine tablets not the good stuff) I was informed that it wasn't her job. It took me an hour of annoying every nurse who came into the ward before I got some painkillers – I was in absolute agony.

Mr Hershman popped in and told me that he had removed a couple of the silver staples that held the hole in my colon together and that everything was fine and there was no infection or swelling from the initial operation. The cancer looked to have gone, the wound was healing well and he should have the official hemotology report back by the end of the month and then we would know definitively whether the operation was a success or not. Obviously I was really happy, and thanked him and asked that he passed my thanks onto Dr Myint. This didn't solve the back pain problem and once again the registrar said that it was referred pain. I'll show you referred pain I mused darkly. I asked whether I could leave as Dad was popping up to see me at two later that afternoon. He wasn't happy about me leaving so soon. I asked him what I needed to do to recover as quickly as possible, and as I had predicted he said to rest and to not move around too much. I pointed out the obvious pitfalls in his argument for keeping me in hospital if that was the case, as I had not slept the last time I was in, nor at all the night before. That being woken at seven every morning was not what I called rest. He finally agreed and I was home by four that afternoon.

Rachel came up for the weekend and all I could manage was to lay on the couch. Whilst I was finding the not knowing what was actually up with me hard, it must have been a nightmare for her. All information was coming in second-hand. She was down in London by herself as most of our friends had disappeared – not just down south but up north as well. Things hadn't been great at home with my extended incapacitation causing stress within the household, and, with Rachel walking into that atmosphere, I just felt for her. She did what she had done all along: kept upbeat in front of me and made me feel better by not judging and just listening – an old door-to-door sales skill. Nod, smile and agree.

The week started as the last one had finished. My bowels just continued to produce the marmalade type stuff; the painkillers were constipating me causing severe stomach cramps which increased the likelihood of me being woken by the morning chorus under the sheets as opposed to the one outside my window. Then I started to get a little more concerned. I was convinced that the pain that was emanating from my lower back wasn't referred but real pain. Sometimes I felt like Mulder from the *X-Files* but in this case the truth was "up there", not out there. I had also started to lose sensation in my extremities. I was getting pins and needles in my legs when I was lying down and would often wake up to a dead arm, butt cheek or leg. I just didn't feel that I was progressing at all after the second hospital visit. The problem was that I didn't know what the problem was and therefore couldn't fix it. Even at my lowest point when receiving chemo and radiotherapy I wasn't this down. I knew the cause of the pain then and could semi-control it.

Now, when going to bed every night, I was begining to experience a completely new sensation, a sensation which had up until that point been alien to me and the way that I had delt with my illness, and that was *Fear*! I hadn't felt fear when they said I had cancer; I hadn't feared during the months of illness and discomfort that I'd gone through with treatment. Nor did I fear the operation, although I knew that it was a risk. Now, I was afraid to go to sleep. Looking back I understand that the amount of morphine I was on was bound to send me off the deep end a little. Nevertheless, I was scared of going to sleep. I was scared of the pain that I would wake up to; I was scared that my dead leg or arm would not wake up. I even got concerned that if my arms, hands and legs were going to sleep then so would my heart. I know it was stupid but I was off my trolly and in some serious pain. I was getting annoyed with myself owing to this internal turmoil and started to despise the person I saw in the mirror in the morning.

On the Thursday, I went to the GP and talked about the back situation. I was in that much agony that I forgot to mention the fact that I was losing sensation in my extremities – muppet. He did what he thought was best and upped my medication because he was convinced that it was also muscular, that I had simply had a bit of a battering and that it wouldn't be long before it sorted intself out. To get around, I had been allowed to use Geoff's late father's walking stick. It was now impossible to walk without support, but of course it was only referred pain – arrrh! The stick did shut me up a bit and made me look at things with a different perspective. Geoff's father had been in Monty's Desert Rats, and those guys knew what pain and despair was all about and I couldn't let my sore back be taken as anything more than that – pull yourself together man! The next day, Mum decided it was time that I got out of the house and we went for a drive. It was a lovely early spring day, so Mum put the roof down and we hurtled off into the countryside. Mum thought that we should go for a spot of lunch and then to see a friend of hers who might be able to help shed some light on the back problem. I was a little self conscious about going to have some lunch out in public, especially with my stick and foam cushion, without which it was impossible for me to sit down. Luckily for me Mum had planned ahead and we went to where the old and the infirm lunch – a garden centre. There were more sticks at this place than a Boy Scouts' fire starter badge day. Cunning. I felt quite nimble on my old pins for the first time in weeks. A cup of tea and a slice of cake later and we were on our way to see Mum's mystery friend. I assumed that it wasn't Santa, so I was intrigued.

Martin lived only a couple of miles away from our house and was a shiatsu master. Shiatsu uses hand pressure and manipulative techniques to adjust the body's *natural inner energies*. Mum said that is can be helpful for conditions like back pain.

The idea was to have someone outside of the traditional medical community have a look at my situation without any preconceived ideas or anything to lose. He saw people at his house and Mum had been to see him a couple of times and raved about how good he was. Before we did anything he made it clear that he would not be actually performing any proceedures on me that day owing to the fact that I had cancer. No external help could be given to me without prior acknowledgement from the surgical or onacological teams. Shiatsu moves the fluids (internal energies) around your system and this was a proper no-no with cancer as you can imagine. So all that we did was have a chat – well, I talked and he listened – for half an hour, and then he asked to take a superficial look at my back. The base of the spine in Chinese medicine is where the adrenalin centre is. The base of my spine was freezing cold and he suggested that this could be an indicator of the fear I felt. He was convinced that there was nerve damage – probably a tear or some other damage to my sciatic nerve. The sciatic nerve originates from five spinal nerve roots: Lumbar nerves L4, L5, and sacral nerves S1, S2, and S3. The sciatic nerve is one of the main nerves in the base of your spine and, if damaged, would explain the loss of sensation in my limbs and why the morphine wasn't helping much as it's not as effective against nerve damage.

It was amazing. I left his house, still in pain and with the stick, but with focus and most importantly a reason why. It didn't matter to me whether he was right or wrong; it seemed plausible and that was good enough for me at that stage of the proceedings. I wanted answers and that one was as good as any. I talked about faith earlier in the book and that is all this was; blind faith with a dash of hope. It was if a huge weight had been lifted and for that I will always be grateful. To paraphrase the great Ricky Tomlinson: *referred pain – my arse*. With that we went home.

It was a rugby weekend on the box, so Geoff and I sat around, drank beer and made plans for an upcoming trip to Benidorm. Mum and Geoff were going to Benidorm on Tuesday 24th with Granddad. Even in his mid eighties he was a nifty dancer and apparently Benidorm is a Mecca for the grey brigade to go and boogie on down. Unfortunately, he had pulled out and seeing as I was in possession of a walking stick it was suggested that a break might do me some good. Our concerns were numerous; not least that I couldn't sit down for two hours on the plane without crawling the walls in pain, and the fact that I was due to have my op at the Linda McCartney ward that morning with the whole gang. We decided that we would go for it anyway. Dad would take me to the clinic whilst Mum and Geoff prepared for the trip and then we would bugger off to Manchester Airport and have a well-deserved week's holiday. It sounded like a plan. By the end of the rugby and beer, we were all agreed that this trip was going to happen, whatever the news about my arse might be.

Come Tuesday morning Dad picked me up at nine and took me down to the clinic for my appointment with both Dr Myint and Hershman at the Linda McCartney ward. I was dreading the clinic; not for the results but for the enforced wait that I was bound to have to endure in the reception without being able to sit or stand with any degree of comfort. I also knew that the good doctors would want to have a manual check and I was not relishing that prospect – not with my back in the state that it was! Right enough, I waited over two hours to be seen and very nearly walked out. I couldn't sit for long, even with the foam cushion the Macmillan nurse Jackie had got me a couple of weeks ago, and standing put pressure on the base of my back. I know it must seem that I was a moaning Minnie, but all I can say in my defence is that I was in as much pain, albeit a different type of pain, with my back as I ever had been when my skin had been burnt black and was falling off owing to the radiotherapy.

I was eventually called into the small examining room, with the bed, and had a chat with the surgical "referred pain" registrar. I was really quite annoyed – not just at the fact that no one had bothered to listen to me at all. Even after going through what I'd been through without bitching, they still didn't believe me when I said that something was wrong. She said that the doctors would go over that. My concern was that either they or she had decided to stick their collective heads in the sand over the back issue because they feared litigation. I don't know if that was the truth but with there being a medical lawsuit in the papers every other week, I had a feeling they were worried that I would have sued them if they turned round and said: "Well we might have damaged a couple of nerves in your back whilst saving your life; take two of these a day, stay lying down and come back in a fortnight." I think that if this was the case, and in retrospect I don't blame them if that was the case, it is sad that denial is the preferred diagnostic tool of the medical administration community, rather than simply making things better. From my point of view it was a no-brainer. Mr Hershman and Dr Myint had gone out of their way to not only try to save my life but save my arse, and if that meant a couple of months with a walking stick because they really got stuck in to remove the entire tumour well Carry On Doctor, as far as I'm concerned.

After a while, the doctors came in with their now mandatory group of trainees, and of course Margaret, to make sure that everyone behaved themselves. My goal for the meeting was to sort the back pain out. The cancer I had forgotten about because that was out of my hands, and I told them so. First off, though, I thanked them both very much for doing what they had done; in spite of criticism from the hospital and other surgeons, they had gone out of their way to help me and whatever the result I was and forever would be in their debt. Mr Hershman just said that they would come to that later. I didn't really catch the solemn undertones in his voice immediately. I just got on with explaining the back situation, how the pain was not referred, how I wasn't that happy about being fobbed off for nearly a month and how a shiatsu practitioner has been the one to make me feel better. Mr Hershman got me on the bed and very carefully examined my back and obviously had to check the actual wound from the surgery. He was more than happy with the internal scarring and said that it had virtually healed and that there was only a very small hole left and once that had closed we were all good. Excellent!

As for the back, he was concerned that mistakes had been made. He explained how it might have happened and agreed that it was damage to the sciatic nerve. He said that I would be given some different drugs to combat the damage. I mentioned that the ora-morph was currently on my toilet cistern owing to the pain that I was in when going to the loo – sit, swig and go! "Nothing like getting high on the bog!" I said. I could still use that for breakthrough pain but he reiterated that painkillers would only bung me up more and therefore make going harder and take more time, which would hurt more, meaning that I'd want more morphine, which would block me up and so on! Not quite the circle of life from the *Lion King*! They also gave me the go-ahead to start swimming and to have the shiatsu done properly.

"Now for the cancer," said Mr Hershman

"Oh!" I said. "I thought that it was all gone."

"Well ... "

"O-Oh!" This was not going to be good or quick by the tone of the conversation so far.

"The basic problem is the depth of the tumour." This didn't sound good, and then he went all technical.

"There are three types of tumour: T1, which is generally a surface tumour on the wall of the colon. T2, which has broken through the colon wall and is on its way to the external wall of the colon; and T3. The T3 type of tumour has breached the wall of the colon and is in danger of moving into the muscle tissue and then escaping into the lymphatic system and the nodes, which are outside the colon itself." The type of surgery that I had received was really designed for polyps and T1 tumours and the occasional T2 with a success rate of 95% and 85% respectively. "Unfortunately, pathology has found that your tumour had gone through both the first and second walls of the colon and had moved into T3 domain. This means that we must recommend the resection operation!"

My mind went: Noooooooooooooooooooooooo!

Then I recovered.

"No!" was my answer.

"The problem is the substance at the base of the tumour, a mucin pool. It is a pool of dead cells, and in this case it is just beyond the muscle wall, which may indicate that the tumour may have previously breached the colon wall prior to surgery. This slop is exactly where the tumour had been," said Dr Myint

"Slop," agreed Mr Hershman, nodding his head.

"Slop?" I queried. "What – like some cancerous goo?"

"Goo. Yes – better description. Goo – like it," said Dr Myint.

What is this, I thought – *Ghostbusters*? "So is goo the technical name now?"

"Yes!" They said in unison.

"The fact is that we have never performed this treatment or operation on a tumour such as yours before and the success rate will have dropped by significantly from a T2."

It's funny what goes through your mind at times like that. Eight months prior to this point I'd thought I had an ulcer, then I was diagnosed with colon cancer, told that if I did nothing I would be dead in less than eighteen months, and that my arse was coming out. Now after months of chemo, radiotherapy, burning, pooing, pain, stress and anguish – not just for me but more importantly for my family and Rachel – they were telling me that the odds of the operation being a success had just dropped from 85% to 50 or 60% even for a T2 tumour. You know what popped into my brain apart from "shit!" It was the scene in *The Empire Strikes Back* where Han Solo flies the Falcon into the asteroid field and C3P0 goes mad saying that the chances of them surviving was X thousand to 1, and Han Solo says "Don't tell me the odds."

"No!" I said. "I'm not prepared to have you rip out my arse on the off chance that some goo might be dodgy – not happening!"

Although they were not a bit surprised by my stance they did reiterate that there was a risk the cancer might come back and that the safest option would be to remove the entire colon and the anus. I was having none of it. I had never lived my life on what ifs and maybes and I wasn't going to sacrifice my bum on an off chance. They took me at my word and set out a five-year plan of check-ups that would start after just six weeks and would be every six weeks for the first two years, then quarterly for the next eighteen months and then every four to six months after that. They were confident that I would be fine but they were not going to allow that confidence get in the way of being safe to the point of maniacal paranoia. Mission accomplished as far as my arse was concerned and that simply left me to thank them again and to pass my thanks to their entire team. We knew that there would be good and bad times ahead and that there was always the risk of it returning because I chose the alternative route. That was a risk that I was happy to live with, and my thoughts about my choice haven't changed today.

Once home I talked with Mum, Dad and Geoff about the results and we all agreed that this was the best course of action and living with "what if" was no way to live. After a while Dad left us to get on with our packing, as we had to be at Manchester Airport within the next couple of hours and Benidorm awaited.

And with that our hero flew off into the sunset – well, clouds, as it was Manchester airport – to start the next chapter in his eventful life and to have a well-deserved holiday.

EPILOGUE: HOW DO YOU SOLVE A PROBLEM LIKE MY REAR?

People ask me all the time, "So how has your life changed?" My life has changed and, in a weird way, I think that getting cancer was the best thing to happen to me. My health is ironically better than it has been since my mid twenties. My diet is better – not great, but better. I still like the odd takeaway and I managed to have my first Singapore noodles on the first anniversary of my being diagnosed with cancer. This was a symbolic gesture as well as it being thirteen months since I'd had any Chinese food, and yes my arse did explode. But it was worth it. I have recently taken up kung fu to keep fit as I'm just not disciplined enough to go to the gym on my own; I get too bored.

The thing that I'm most happy about, apart from not dying and not having my bum removed, is that my relationship with my dad, as an adult-to-adult relationship, has never been better. I go walking in the lakes with him and his DOM. brigade: Dirty Old Men, twenty, crazy, sixty- year-old-plus blokes. Hilarious. I've worked with him and see him more than I have for twenty years. My relationship with my mum is as strong as ever – more like mates than Mum and son – and I have got engaged to Rachel. Any girl who can put up with what she had to deserves nothing less. Still haven't got many mates though! There are other things that I wasn't expecting, like the fact that I can type a lot quicker than I could prior to be ill. Whether I type anything worth reading is a subject of debate. I sit down to wee 75% of the time – better to be on the safe side as far as my pants are concerned. My psoriasis has returned, especially on my head. If my hair fell out now I'm sure that I'd look like Michael

Gambon in Denis Potter's *The Singing Detective*. I have subsequently tried every trick in the book from Chinese medicine; this consists of bags of what can only be described as twigs being boiled up, and then the liquid drunk. It cost hundreds of pounds and didn't work at all – although we never had any mosquitoes in the house for months.

I was also lucky enough to be able to go on holiday a couple of times during 2004 and I noticed that the photosensitivity of the chemo was still in my system. My skin also seemed to be more photosensitive and when in really hot places the skin on the back of my hands blistered red like a really bad sun or nettle rash. This was due, I think, to the chemo although my oncologist insists that this is not the case, although it had never happened before the chemo and four years on it still happens, although to a lesser extent. There are other things that the doctors have assured me bear no relation to the treatment, but nevertheless they still occur. When I'm down or stressed I get the target lesions that I had for the first time in the early chemo days. I periodically get a patch of cold-sore-like blisters, about the size of ten pence coins, on the back of my thigh – approximately where my leg was in contact with toilet seats. Doctors said that it couldn't be cold sores as they don't manifest themselves there. Again, that hasn't stopped them returning a couple of times a year. One of the side-effects that I wasn't aware of from chemo is the propensity to cry more – I'm now an emotional wreck. I well up at anything. Especially happy stuff or when people excel through talent or hit their dreams – I even get emotional when watching *X Factor*, when the person really hits the mark.

Also, after the battering that my mouth took during chemo, with all the cold sores and ulcers, I now have real issues with drinking hot liquids. I literally have to make the coffee in the morning before getting in the shower – only when I get out can I even attempt to drink it. Aside from my mouth, the rest of my body seems to have lost all sense of climate control. When it's cool I'll be sweating buckets and when it's hot, more often than not, I'm like the Wicked Witch of the West post-water! I've yet to find an antiperspirant which works – suggestions welcome!

"What about the past couple of years?" I hear you cry. (Of course the cry could just be happiness that the book is nearly finished.) Although my back was not good after the operation and I did not stop using the stick until May, this didn't stop me having a bit of a ball for the rest of 2004. Upon returning home to London, I was again fortunate to have the aid of the Macmillan cancer support nurses who helped with everything from massage for my back, to trying to persuade my local council that the cancer wasn't a joke and that I was not a member of the Taliban – although that might have got me some support, that or hijacking a plane. Sorry – still annoyed! I also travelled. The holiday in Benidorm with Mum and Geoff was a great tonic and so I made sure that 2004 was the year of the holiday. Dad paid for Rachel and I to go over to an all-inclusive resort in the Dominican Republic at the end of April, which was fantastic. Then, at the end of May, Rob decided that he and I should go away for a boys' week to Zante (one of the Greek islands) which was also a bit of a giggle – especially my Speedo and cowboy boots pool run. After the summer and with my back fully recovered, I went to see Ben in Bali for a couple of weeks. I met some great people on all of these holidays, both Brits and locals alike and the one thing that was resoundingly obvious to me was that we are all the same. No matter where you are from, what your colour or religion is, people are people when it comes down to the individual, and cancer is a global concern for all.

The thing that I started to struggle with though was not the financial, physical or mental pressure that having cancer can put you under, but the perceived social pressures. Having cancer for me was quite easy mentally; not having it was, for me anyway, harder. From when I was diagnosed and throughout my treatment, I always had immediate goals and things to be getting on with. Without sounding vain and spoilt, you are the centre of attention and people are actively nice to you. Once that short-term threat had been removed, however, people's expectations seemed to change. Firstly, what do you say your situation is? With colon cancer, even with my slightly more risky operation, there is no remission as such – it's there or it's not. It's not like some of the hardcore cancers where remission can be just that – an interlude between treatments. The great thing about this cancer is that if it is diagnosed and treated soon enough it can be cured. So I didn't have cancer, which was a good thing, although it could return, but not in the same way as say leukaemia might.

Expectations are that it's like your eyes being opened to the beauty of the world for the first time – and to a certain extent that is true. I made sure that I tried to see as much of the countries that I travelled to as possible, their culture and their heritage. Be that, by visiting temples in Indonesia and Malaysia, or simply taking in the view over Windermere in the Lakes. It's the realities of life that people seemed to neglect to mention or forget about. I had no job to throw myself back into and so had no routine for a long time, as getting a job was very difficult – keeping one often proved harder as I found myself with less, not more, patience. I don't mean getting stressed on the tube or in traffic; if you can't do anything why panic has always been my mentality – circle of influence and all that. What I mean is that I have found myself getting impatient with people, especially idiots. I don't know if subconsciously I'm scared of wasting time on them because it seems that I swing from one life-threatening dilemma to the next. Perhaps I'm simply scared for how much time I might have before the next disaster and I don't see why I should waste it on muppets. Once cured, or not as is often the case, it seems that you're expected to go off fund-raising and run marathons, help old people and animals and all that sort of stuff when in reality I just keep finding myself getting angry at the world and wanting to give it a shake. I still had my bills to pay, bosses to answer to, and life to live, but I feel that I look at the world in a more macro not micro point of view. I worry about the way that we are driving the planet to the edge of oblivion and the only people who seem to have noticed at all is the lefty tree-huggers and the looneys. I have often thought about maybe getting into politics, but I've had more than three sexual relationships and I most definitely did inhale. Luckily since my illness things like climate change have become big business and if there is a PR angle it'.

I'm sure I'm not the only person who has found living harder than the prospect of dying. The Reaper does focus the mind somewhat. I don't really want you to think that I have gone off the deep end because I haven't. I moved up north with Rachel, near Manchester, which is closer to my parents and the hospital, at the end of 2006. The drop in the pace of life, from being smack bang in the centre of London, is a nice change. I still get a kick out of the little things in life like going for a bike ride, getting a new Xbox game or simply hanging out with mates. I still like Stella and I still like to have the odd Chinese – especially Singapore Noodles. I live to the motto "I didn't die, so I don't want to stop living" – and that gets me up every.

All that said and done I am very glad to be alive and still be able to read the Sunday papers on the loo, not next to it. I am, and will always be, eternally grateful to all of the staff and doctors at Homerton, Barts, Clatterbridge, RLH, Arrow Park and all of the other places where they have wanted to stick their fingers up my arse. I have passed the two- and the four-year watersheds of my rehabilitation and just as Mr Hershman and Doctor Myint hoped, all is well with my bum. I still produce enough gas to cause holes in the ozone layer and go to the loo at least five times a day but hey what's the odd fart between friends?I hope that anyone who reads this takes something from it, even if that's only: that Mark bloke is a bit weird. Cancer is scary but not as scary as I had thought. The bravest people I have ever met, I met in cancer wards and they shamed me with their strength and humour on many an occasion, when I felt mine beginning to crumble. More people live long and happy lives after having cancer then ever before and those who don't go down fighting. This is a nightmare illness but from that nightmare come some amazing stories of strength and courage. It's just a shame that, as a species, we are at our best when things are at their worst.

I have to go now because I need a poo!

The End